The Essential Mary Parker Follett:

Ideas We Need Today

Edited by
François Héon, Albie Davis,
Jennifer Jones-Patulli, Sébastien Damart

Published by François Héon (Inc.), Albie Davis, Jennifer Jones-Patulli, and Sébastien Damart.

Copyright © 2017, second edition. François Héon, Albie Davis, Jennifer Jones-Patulli, and Sébastien Damart.

All rights reserved. No part of this publication may be reproduced, distributed, or transmitted in any form or by any means, including photocopying, recording, or other electronic or mechanical methods, without the prior written permission of the publisher, except in the case of brief quotations embodied in critical reviews and certain other non-commercial uses permitted by copyright law.

For permission requests, write to the editors:

E. fheon@francoisheon.com | www.francoisheon.com

ISBN: 978-0-9939553-0-3

Library and Archives Canada Cataloguing in Publication
Follett, Mary Parker, 1868-1933 [Works. Selections]

The Essential Mary Parker Follett / edited by François Héon, Albie Davis, Jennifer Jones-Patulli, Sébastien Damart. -- Second edition.

Includes bibliographical references.
ISBN 978-0-9939553-0-3 (pbk.)

1. Organization. 2. Individuality. 3. Leadership. 4. Democracy. 5. Social structure. 6. Management.

I. Davis, Albie M., editor II. Damart, Sébastien, editor III. Héon, François, 1965-, editor IV. Jones-Patulli, Jennifer, 1978-, editor V. Title.

HM796.F65 2014   302.3'5   C2014-907161-2

Cover design: Carole Zabbal-Wynne in collaboration with Albie Davis and Christopher Pino.

Front cover image credit: NASA Earth Observatory image by Robert Simmon, using Suomi NPP VIIRS imagery from NOAA's Environmental Visualization Laboratory. Suomi NPP is the result of a partnership between NASA, NOAA and the Department of Defense. Caption by Mike Carlowicz.

Back cover image credit: NASA Goddard Space Flight Center Image by Reto Stöckli (land surface, shallow water, clouds). Enhancements by Robert Simmon (ocean color, compositing, 3D globes, animation). Data and technical support: MODIS Land Group; MODIS Science Data Support Team; MODIS Atmosphere Group; MODIS Ocean Group Additional data: USGS EROS Data Center (topography); USGS Terrestrial Remote Sensing Flagstaff Field Center (Antarctica); Defense Meteorological Satellite Program (city lights).

An important and long-overdue contribution to management literature

"This is an important and long overdue contribution to management literature; one to which every MBA student should be exposed. In resurrecting and organizing the profound insights of Mary Parker Follett, the editors have reconnected us with a pioneering thought leader whose voice has been lost or subdued for way too long. Careful reading will demonstrate the gift the editors have provided in revealing the root ideas behind much of today's post-modern approaches to managing and organizing human behavior."

— Ronald Fry, PhD
Professor of Organizational Behavior,
Case Western Reserve University

A book that stands out for its depth, message, simplicity and impact

"In an era supercharged by social media where surface level understanding is all that is often visible, this collection by François Héon, Albie Davis, Jennifer Jones-Patulli and Sébastien Damart stands out for its depth, message, simplicity, and impact. I find their work highly appealing in celebrating the forgotten work of one the most original organizational theorists."

— Tojo Thatchenkery, PhD
Professor and Director,
Organization Development & Knowledge Management
George Mason University,
co-author of
Appreciative Intelligence: Seeing the Mighty Oak in the Acorn

A perfectly timed revival of Mary Parker Follett's thought

"This revival of Mary Parker Follett's thought is perfectly timed for the challenges of 21st-century leadership. Her emphasis on experiential learning, team work, collaborative problem-solving and conflict resolution are more important than ever for today's dynamic, changing organizations."

— David A. Kolb, PhD
Founder and Chairman,
Experience Based Learning Systems, Inc.
www.learningfromexperience.com

Of all those who, in our own time, have devoted intellect and effort to the examination of the problem of organization, Mary Follett was the most original and the most suggestive. ... It will be a grave misfortune if her lucid and illuminating ideas about organization do not become part of the thought of all those who are interested in administration. They were, they are, perhaps a little ahead of her time and of the present. But they are a gold mine of suggestion for anyone who wants to think clearly about this subject. And they are presented with that beautiful simplicity which is the highest art.

– Lyndall Urwick
British management consultant and business thinker

Bulletin of The Taylor Society
and of The Society of Industrial Engineers, 1935.

Table of contents

Introduction..1
   About Mary Parker Follett 3
   A Gifted Student 4
   Early Civic Activity 6
   Work with Businessmen 7
   A Pragmatist at Heart 10
   Her Relevance Today 12
   Five Themes 13

1. Mary Parker Follett on Valuing Differences. 18
   Differences are the Seeds of Creativity 23
   Uniting through Diversity.................................30
   Integrating Differences within Ourselves 37
   The Difference of Every Moment 45
   Differences Make the World Go Round............53

2. Mary Parker Follett on Group Organization 62
   Group Organization as a New Method 66
   Group Process is a Creative Process 70
   Group Organization vs. Crowd Organization....81
   The Group, the Leader and Power....................93
   Group Organization as a Practice 98
   The Technique of Democracy
   is Group Organization 101

**3. Mary Parker Follett on the Process
of Integration**... 106
   The Creative Intelligence of Integration 110
   Constructive Conflict through Integration......120
   Integration Goes Beyond Compromise 125

Living Integration 129
Integration and the Circular Response 141
Experiencing Power and Democracy
through Integration 146

4. Mary Parker Follett on Leadership 158
Leadership as Integrating 163
Following the Invisible Leader 173
Finding the Law of the Situation 180
Leading is Power-With 185
Empowering Functional Leadership 198
Leading by Example 205
Leaders Develop Leaders 208
Leadership and Collective Creativity 214

5. Mary Parker Follett on Democracy 220
New Method, New Democracy........................224
Learning Democracy 235
Creating Rather than Following 237
Democracy, Patriotism and Loyalty 249
Living Democracy 255

Bibliography 259

Acknowledgments 260

A special thank you 263

About the Editors 265

Introduction

When our Follett Writing Team met at Northeastern University in Boston for the first Mary Parker Follett Conversations in the fall of 2011, only two of our five members were already acquainted. The rest of us were "strangers" to each other, although we had corresponded over the internet to help plan the event. Our conversations icebreaker started with the metaphorical question, "How did you meet Mary Parker Follett?"

Fascinating stories emerged. We had all been struck by her intelligence, and her words lifted our spirits. Mary Parker Follett gave us the clues and confidence we needed to invent and explore new ways of approaching mediation, management, leadership, democracy, life.

Using an integrative process, we embarked as a group of Follett enthusiasts on a two-year collaborative effort to select the best Follett passages we could find.

The purpose of this book is to provide a doorway into Follett's thoughts – it is deliberately not a scholarly work. Following in Follett's footsteps, we tried to create a work that has practical application and can be used across a wide range of fields. Readers are invited to open to any page and ponder a thought or idea as long as they wish. For those who want to better understand the breadth of her thinking, each of the five themes has also been sub-divided into sub-themes to facilitate a more continuous reading.

As we developed this book, we were struck by the aesthetic of much of her writing. Some of the following quotes read like poems, singing gracefully in the mind's ear. It is our wish that these words captivate you with their wisdom and grace, as much as they did us, and as much as they did more than 100 years ago in Follett's day.

The Follett Team
Rouen ~ Montreal ~ Boston
October 2014

About Mary Parker Follett

Most people who learn about Follett quite naturally begin to associate her through their own lens on life. Her work applies to many professions – management consultant, political scientist, teacher, community leader and mediator, to name just a few. If she were sending out her résumé in our era, she could rightly call herself any of these vocations. But her life's quest was to find universal principles of human interaction and creativity that could apply to all endeavours.

She was born in 1868 in Quincy, Massachusetts, a child of the Civil War growing up in New England. A voracious reader and extraordinary student, she excelled in grammar school, being the youngest student of her day admitted into Thayer Academy in nearby Braintree. While there, she thrived under the guidance of a brilliant and demanding teacher, Anna Boynton Thompson, who would remain a lifelong friend.

As a young woman, Follett went on to study at the Society for the Collegiate Instruction of Women, nicknamed the "Harvard Annex", which drew upon volunteer Harvard professors to teach classes. During her time there, the Annex was chartered as Radcliffe College. In 1999, the college would officially merge with Harvard University to become the Radcliffe Institute for Advanced Study at Harvard University.

A Gifted Student

She enjoyed remarkable success in academia. It was an exciting time in Cambridge, known as Harvard's "Golden Age" of philosophy, with Royce, Santayana, Münsterberg, James and Palmer as its leading lights. She mingled with a fascinating and diverse group of students and studied under the guidance of eminent professors. She took classes in history, government, political economy, French, Latin and German. While on a year abroad at Newnham College in Cambridge, England, her most memorable experience was one small, personalized seminar on the history of political theory with Professor Henry Sidgwick, founder of Newnham. The class initially had two students; when one of the students dropped out, Sidgwick continued his lectures for Follett alone. Follett called her year at Newnham the great milepost and turning point in her life.

Her own works integrated notions from fields as varied as philosophy, political theory, biology, psychology, law, economics, mathematics, social science, physics, engineering, art and the emerging field of business as a profession. She was influenced by a range of theoretical ideas, from German idealism to American pragmatism.

Her published thesis *The Speaker of the House of Representatives*, written for a history course taught by Albert Bushnell Hart, earned her a place among Radcliffe's fifty most distinguished graduates. Theodore Roosevelt, New York City's police commissioner at the time, reviewed the work, saying she "has made a really notable contribution to the study of the growth of American governmental institutions," and called it "marvelously well done."[i] The *New York Times* listed it among "The Fifty Best Books of 1896."[ii] By 1898, she graduated *summa cum laude* alongside other such contemporary luminaries as poet and writer Gertrude Stein.

Early Civic Activity

In 1894, Follett met Isobel Briggs, the principal of a private day school in Boston's Back Bay, founded by an activist philanthropist, Pauline Agassiz Shaw. Briggs and Follett would spend the next 30 years together in a loving and devoted relationship, sharing a rented apartment in Beacon Hill and spending their summers at a cottage they commissioned to be built in Putney, Vermont.

Beyond her academic importance, Follett was a pioneer in civic organizing and community education. She is generally regarded as the "primary architect of the Boston school centers movement,"[iii] successfully lobbying and fundraising for schools to remain open after-hours. This creative initiative brought together various public departments to collaborate and allow Boston citizens – particularly newly arrived immigrants – to participate in self-managed community activities. She was later voted in unanimously as the first vice president of the National Community Centers Association in the United States.[iv]

Her work on civic projects, notably the Boston Placement Bureau, brought her in contact with some of the leading businessmen of the day. It was there she met Henry Dennison, who was then serving as representative for the Boston Chamber of Commerce.

In late 1925, Briggs was diagnosed with cancer and died within weeks. Deep in mourning, Follett threw herself into her work, continuing her studies with characteristic fervour, but with a renewed purpose. Her book *Creative Experience*, published the previous year, had prompted a flood of requests from businessmen seeking her out for both public lectures and private counsel.[v]

Work with Businessmen

Henry C. Metcalf deserves credit for recognizing Follett's gift of speaking to the minds and hearts of businessmen. Follett and Metcalf had worked together in Boston on vocational issues. In 1924, he invited her to speak the following year at the Bureau of Personnel Administration (BPA), which he founded. Her topic was Constructive Conflict and from the start, she captured her audience. The word spread. She received many requests for private consultations. She gave a total of 14 such lectures on various topics over the period of four years. Then, after an absence, she presented her last lecture in 1932,"The Individual in a Planned Society", reflecting the impact of the Great Depression.

By 1926, Follett decided to devote herself to the study of business management. "It is among business men (not all, but a few) that I find the greatest vitality of thinking to-day, and I like to do my thinking where it is most alive,"[vi] she stated.

Seebohm Rowntree, a British social reformer and industrialist, who met Follett during his own 1921 lecture tour in the United States, invited Follett to give three talks in 1926 at a conference for "Works Directors, Managers, Foremen and Forewomen," held at Balliol College in Oxford. It is there that she met Lyndall Urwick (see page iv) who became her most ardent admirer and advocate. Urwick arranged for Follett to give a series of talks at the inauguration of the Business Administration Department of the London School of Economics in early 1933.

After her death in December 1933, Urwick and Metcalf collaborated on publishing *Dynamic Administration: The Collected Papers of Mary Parker Follett* (1941). And in 1949, Urwick had her talks at the London School of Economics published as *Freedom &*

Co-ordination: Lectures in Business Organization.

Follett eventually moved to England, where she spent her remaining years with Dame Katharine Furse, whom she had met while observing the League of Nations in Geneva. Furse, first head of Women's Royal Naval Service (WRNS) was Head of the World Association of Girl Guides and Girl Scouts when they first met.

In late November 1933, Follett returned to the U.S. to tend to financial matters and for a second opinion about her health, which had been cause for concern for some time. She took a turn for the worse and died in Boston, following an operation, on December 18, 1933.

Her friends, Henry and Mary Dennison, drove to Vermont and scattered her ashes near Follett's summer home, Overhills, where she loved to watch the sunset.

A Pragmatist at Heart

Those who knew Mary Parker Follett well were the first to recognize her unique ability to listen intently. People from all walks of life, from the man on the factory floor and the shop girl in a department store to the president of a major corporation, felt at ease in her presence. Everyone was made to feel that their contribution was a vital part of the whole. That holistic approach is a core element of Follett's philosophy: for her, every voice counts. Follett believed in our human capacity to invent the way we organize our lives and institutions so each individual can contribute and develop their full creative potential in the process.

The breadth and depth of her thinking is well exemplified in her call to a life of *progressive integratings; integratings* which she proposes begin at the intrapersonal level, and extend to the interpersonal, local, national and international levels as well. Her life and works reflect a profound appreciation for the active and iterative processes of productive human interaction: those interactions that enliven human relationships, whether they take place at the kitchen or the boardroom table.

But while Follett may have been a brilliant theoretician, she purposely did not offer any "-isms". Instead of the "-ism", she offers us the "-ing": engaging, creating, integrating, doing, living. She was adamantly pragmatic in her thinking.

Lyndall Urwick puts it aptly:

> *While she thus made political science the subject of her first choice and the theme of prolonged and incessant academic research, her attitude was always emphatically experimental and practical. She had no trace of the academic fallacy about her, no hint that learning is for learning's sake. She thirsted for knowledge, but always for the enlargement of life.*[vii]

Follett both conformed to some of the norms of her day, and ignored others. In some cases, she did both. For example, most often she used the masculine noun as the normative expression meaning "all people." Yet, a word usage scan of her writing shows she periodically reminds her readers that if she's been using men most often, she means everyone by using such expressions as "men and women, husbands and wives, mothers and fathers, boys and girls," and so forth. Our team of two women and two men agree we feel it best to let readers experience Follett in her own voice.

Her Relevance Today

As we move ahead in the 21st century, her work is more relevant than ever. We are seeing a similar level of ground-shifting change to that of her era in technology, globalization, the migration of different peoples, and the struggle for more effective democracies around the world.

The challenge and opportunity of integrating our differences remains fundamental. How do we integrate our individual differences within our families? How do we creatively integrate our diverse interests and needs within our public institutions or private corporations? Or how do we, together, constructively integrate the diversity of cultures and belief systems throughout our world?

New technology has ushered in new opportunities for togetherness, but technology has not and will not deliver us from the human challenge and opportunity of uniting our differences in creative ways. Unifying our individual wills and becoming something more is our own work, and Mary Parker Follett offers us practical wisdom on how to do this. She called it Living Democracy.

Five Themes

We organized Follett's main ideas under the following five themes.

Valuing Differences

Follett believed that every individual's voice was essential to democracy. The differences among people, and the ensuing conflict, were the seeds of innovation. She shows us how differences arising from a single individual, a family, a neighborhood, a nation or internationally can nurture creativity, personal development, social progress and true democracy. We must learn to seek and embrace difference, not fear and avoid it.

Group Organization

Follett presents group organizing as the basic process of social organization, democracy and personal development. She calls group organization the method of coordination and affirms its creative potential for the group and the individual.

The Process of Integration

The process of integration is at the heart of Follett's philosophy. It is for this reason that we positioned this theme in the middle and at the heart of the book. Integration builds on differences. It goes beyond positions to uncover true interests and to elicit genuine dialogue among participants. Integration is the meeting of differences, to create something new – thus preserving the integrity of the individual.

Leadership

The capacity for humans to be willful co-creators of their lives makes leadership a key method according to Follett for personal and collective development. Her avant-garde notions of *power-with management*, *obeying the law of the situation* or of *following the invisible leader*, are some examples of a leadership philosophy that remains as relevant as ever.

Democracy

Follett defines democracy as the 'genuine union of true individuals'. Her ideas, brought together from various disciplines, provide a framework that can be applied to leadership, group organization and democracy as a whole. The individual is not subsumed by the group in democracy, but rather is affirmed. Democracy invites us to become more complete individuals as we co-create our worlds.

Timeline ~ Mary P. Follett's Era

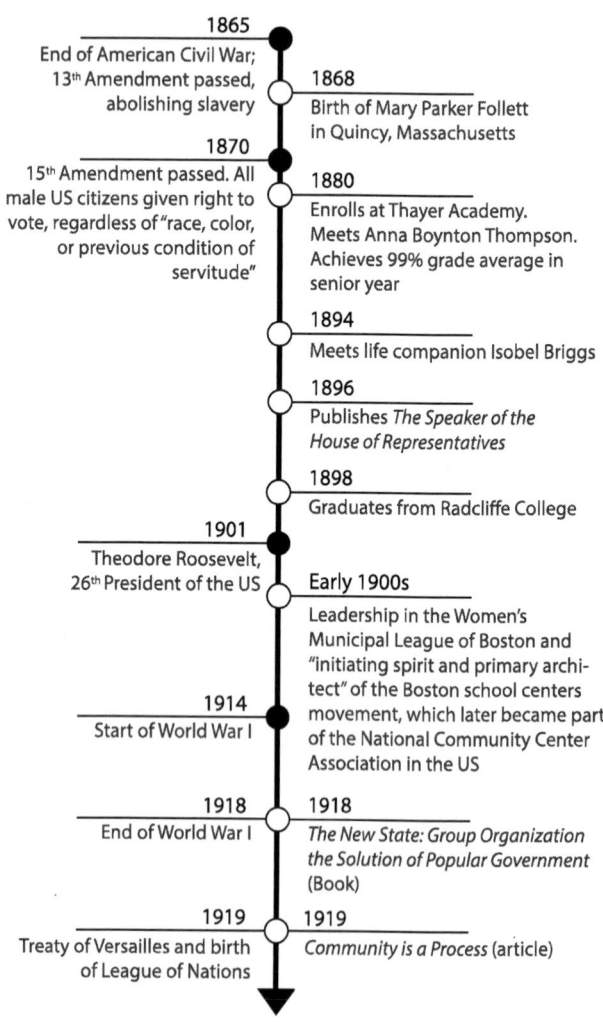

1865
End of American Civil War; 13th Amendment passed, abolishing slavery

1868
Birth of Mary Parker Follett in Quincy, Massachusetts

1870
15th Amendment passed. All male US citizens given right to vote, regardless of "race, color, or previous condition of servitude"

1880
Enrolls at Thayer Academy. Meets Anna Boynton Thompson. Achieves 99% grade average in senior year

1894
Meets life companion Isobel Briggs

1896
Publishes *The Speaker of the House of Representatives*

1898
Graduates from Radcliffe College

1901
Theodore Roosevelt, 26th President of the US

Early 1900s
Leadership in the Women's Municipal League of Boston and "initiating spirit and primary architect" of the Boston school centers movement, which later became part of the National Community Center Association in the US

1914
Start of World War I

1918
End of World War I

1918
The New State: Group Organization the Solution of Popular Government (Book)

1919
Treaty of Versailles and birth of League of Nations

1919
Community is a Process (article)

Timeline ~ Mary P. Follett's Era

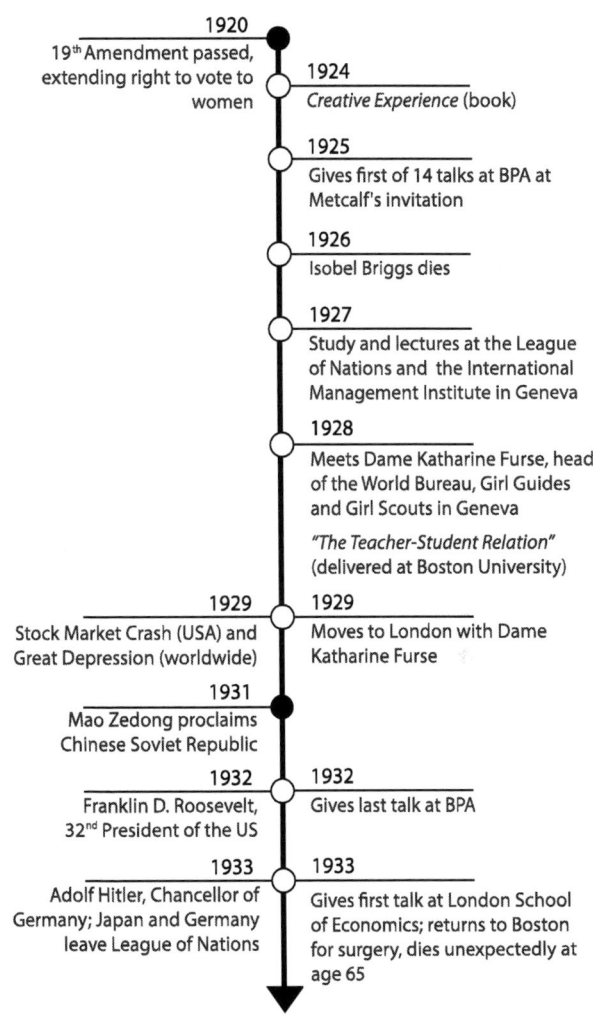

1920 — 19th Amendment passed, extending right to vote to women

1924 — *Creative Experience* (book)

1925 — Gives first of 14 talks at BPA at Metcalf's invitation

1926 — Isobel Briggs dies

1927 — Study and lectures at the League of Nations and the International Management Institute in Geneva

1928 — Meets Dame Katharine Furse, head of the World Bureau, Girl Guides and Girl Scouts in Geneva

"The Teacher-Student Relation" (delivered at Boston University)

1929 — Stock Market Crash (USA) and Great Depression (worldwide)

1929 — Moves to London with Dame Katharine Furse

1931 — Mao Zedong proclaims Chinese Soviet Republic

1932 — Franklin D. Roosevelt, 32nd President of the US

1932 — Gives last talk at BPA

1933 — Adolf Hitler, Chancellor of Germany; Japan and Germany leave League of Nations

1933 — Gives first talk at London School of Economics; returns to Boston for surgery, dies unexpectedly at age 65

Notes

i   Roosevelt, Theodore. *Review of The Speaker of the House of Representatives*, M. P. Follett. *American Historical Review*, Vol. 2, October 1, 1896. http://archive.org/details/jstor-1833641

ii   "The Fifty Best Books of 1896," *New York Times*, June 5, 1897.

iii   Tonn, Joan C. *Mary P. Follett: Creating Democracy, Transforming Management* (New Haven and London: Yale University Press, 2003), 204.

iv   *Ibid.*, 250.

v   *Ibid.*, 388.

vi   *Ibid.*, 388.

vii   "The Problem of Organization: A Study of the Work of Mary Parker Follett." *Bulletin of The Taylor Society and of The Society of Industrial Engineers as Members of Federated Management Societies* I (July 1935): 163-64.

Mary Parker Follett on Valuing Differences

"Fear of difference is dread of life itself."
~CE30

Not one to avoid life, this American woman left the academic world in which she was so successful and went to work in Boston's neighborhoods. There was plenty to be done. Since Follett's birth in 1868, the population in the Boston area had grown tenfold. Waves of newcomers seeking a "better life" came from Ireland, Canada, Russia, Italy and Germany, and, in time, from America's Deep South, settling in "the city on the hill," most often in crowded tenements. The great majority of immigrants came with the clothes on their back and very little else.

Follett worked at Boston's grassroots level for twenty years, initiating a citywide program to open neighborhood schools to all residents in the evenings. These publicly sponsored Evening Centers were specifically designed to be run by neighbors, for neighbors. As she worked alongside people from all backgrounds, watching them planning programs, making budget decisions, attending and analyzing classes and learning how to improve their Center's offerings, she clearly saw how central diversity was to a vibrant democracy.

She also learned that when people expressed their differences, sparks flew, and thus people often avoided talking about anything controversial. By doing so, they missed the opportunity to creatively use their many points of view to create something new. She developed an entirely new approach toward conflict, which allowed people to move through various stages identifying and integrating interests so they could come up with solutions that met everyone's needs.

Whenever she observed a tendency that seemed counter-productive or even destructive, she found a new way to look at it, sometimes overturning a commonly held notion. One example is her conclusion about the concept of evil: "Evil is non-relation." (NS62-63). That is, evil does not reside in this person or that person, but in the fact they are cut off from one another. If, as fellow citizens on Earth, we put this thought into action, we might let go of the ultimately dangerous definition of differences, one that allows us to set aside our shared humanity and instead sort people into categories where some are good and others are evil.

This section illustrates how Follett's ever-growing understanding of the power of difference helped her "break the code" to discover the true nature of conflict. Once you can appreciate the power of differences, see them as natural sources of "conflict", and appreciate the nourishment their interplay provides, you see them in a new light. In doing so herself, she discovered the following:

1. Differences are the seeds of creativity

Once the fear of difference is abandoned and conflict is no longer automatically feared, avoided or suppressed, the creative force of differences is free to spark the continuous process of innovation and evolution.

2. Uniting through diversity

As people work together, every person offers ideas and, in turn, opens up to new influences; unity is nurtured by the very process of exploring differences. By integrating differences into something new, each individual and group grows.

3. Integrating differences within ourselves

Consider how often we are not able to make up our minds, because we are of two minds, or even three or four. These internal differences, when recognized, can become part of the creative mix towards wholeness.

4. The difference of every moment

Life is ever-changing. Follett reminds us of the human capacity to willfully participate in co-creating the next moment.

5. Differences make the world go round

The differences among the many cultures in our world enrich all of our lives. Just as our families, communities and countries grow strong thanks to diversity, so does our world.

1 Differences are the Seeds of Creativity

Differences are the Seeds of Creativity

"At the outset I should like to ask you to agree for the moment to think of conflict as neither good nor bad; to consider it without ethical pre-judgment; to think of it not as warfare, but as the appearance of difference, difference of opinions, of interests. For that is what conflict means – difference. We shall not consider merely the differences between employer and employee, but those between managers, between the directors at the Board meetings, or wherever difference appears."
~DA30

Differences are the Seeds of Creativity

"As conflict – difference – is here in this world, as we cannot avoid it, we should, I think, use it. Instead of condemning it, we should set it to work for us. Why not? What does the mechanical engineer do with friction? Of course his chief job is to eliminate friction, but it is true that he also capitalizes on friction. The transmission of power by belts depends on friction between the belt and the pulley. The friction between the driving wheel of the locomotive and the track is necessary to haul the train. All polishing is done by friction. The music of the violin we get by friction. We left the savage state when we discovered fire by friction. We talk of the friction of mind on mind as a good thing. So in business too, we have to know when to try to eliminate friction and when to try to capitalize it, when to see what work we can make it do. That is what I wish to consider here, whether we can set conflict to work and make it do something for us."

~DA30-31

Differences are the Seeds of Creativity

"What people often mean by getting rid of conflict is getting rid of diversity, and it is of the utmost importance that these should not be considered the same. We may wish to abolish conflict, but we cannot get rid of diversity. We must face life as it is and understand that diversity is its most essential feature. Fear of difference is dread of life itself. It is possible to conceive of conflict as not necessarily a wasteful outbreak of incompatibilities, but a normal process by which socially valuable differences register themselves for the enrichment of all concerned."

~CE300-301

Differences are the Seeds of Creativity

"Instead of shutting out what is different, we should welcome it because it is different and through its difference will make a richer content of life. The ignoring of differences is the most fatal mistake in politics or industry or international life: every difference that is swept up into a bigger conception feeds and enriches society; every difference which is ignored feeds *on* society and eventually corrupts it."
~DA40

Differences are the Seeds of Creativity

"The confronting of diverse desires, the thereby revealing of 'values,' the consequent revaluation of values, a uniting of desires which we welcome above all because it means that the next diversity will emerge on a higher social level – this is progress."
~CExiv

Differences are the Seeds of Creativity

"A new being springs forth from every fresh contact. My nature opens and opens to thousands of new influences. I feel countless new births. Such is the glory of our common every-day life."
~NS38

1 UNITING THROUGH DIVERSITY

Uniting through Diversity

"Unity, not uniformity, must be our aim. We attain unity only through variety. Differences must be integrated, not annihilated, nor absorbed. Anarchy means unorganized, unrelated difference; coordinated, unified difference belongs to our ideal of a perfect social order. We don't want to avoid our adversary but to 'agree with him quickly'; we must, however, learn the technique of agreeing."

~NS39

"As long as we think of difference as that which divides us, we shall dislike it; when we think of it as that which unites us, we shall cherish it."
~NS39-40

"Give your difference, welcome my difference, unify all difference in the larger whole – such is the law of growth. The unifying of difference is the eternal process of life – the creative synthesis, the highest act of creation, the at-onement. The implications of this conception when we come to define democracy are profound."

~NS40

"Our 'opponents' are our co-creators, for they have something to give which we have not."
~CE174

"We could not have an enemy unless there was much in common between us. Differences are always grounded in an underlying similarity."
~NS36

"We must remember that most people are not for or against anything; the first object of getting people together is to make them respond somehow, to overcome inertia. To disagree, as well as to agree, with people brings you closer to them. I always feel intimate with my enemies. It is not opposition but indifference which separates men."
~NS212

Uniting through Diversity

"Each must discover and contribute that which distinguishes him from others, his difference. The only use for my difference is to join it with other differences. The unifying of opposites is the eternal process. We must have an imagination which will leap from the particular to the universal. Our joy, our satisfaction, must always be in the more inclusive aspect of our problem."
~NS29

1 INTEGRATING DIFFERENCES WITHIN OURSELVES

Integrating Differences within Ourselves

"We must stop here, however, to remind ourselves of something we all know well – that before anyone can learn how to be a worthy and effective member of society, before he can take in social integration, he must have learned to integrate the different tendencies in himself."
~TS11

Integrating Differences within Ourselves

"When we have conflicts, or differences of opinion, between two individuals – employer and employee, or two executives, or two members of a board of directors – it is not only our task to try to reconcile these two individuals. We have to study each individual to see if there are not, perhaps, diverse tendencies warring with each other within the individual, for this internal conflict may be the very thing which will prevent a satisfactory settling of the conflict between these individuals. We have, moreover, to see what measures we can take to reconcile these warring tendencies, to resolve the internal conflict, in order that these individuals can enter into effective relations with each other. But we must remember, what is sometimes forgotten, that this is not an antecedent process; the two integrations are simultaneous."

~DA203

Integrating Differences within Ourselves

"The conflict between A and B, or the integrating between A and B, may help A to unify the diverse tendencies in himself, may help B to do the same. These are not really two processes, but one; the individual would not be integrating his personality if he lived in a world by himself. It is exactly the same kind of a double process as that which I gave you in my illustration from the marketing co-operatives."
~DA203

Integrating Differences within Ourselves

"Psychology has given us the phrase 'progressive integratings'; we need also the phrase progressive differings. We can often measure our progress by watching the nature of our conflicts. Social progress is in this respect like individual progress; we become spiritually more and more developed as our conflicts rise to higher levels. If a man should tell you that his chief daily conflict within himself is – Shall I steal or not steal? You would know what to think of his stage of development. As someone has said, 'A man is known by the dilemmas he keeps.' In the same way, one test of your business organization is not how many conflicts you have, for conflicts are the essence of life, but what are your conflicts? And how do you deal with them? It is to be hoped that we shall not always have strikes, but it is equally to be hoped that we shall always have conflict, the kind which leads to invention, to the emergence of new values."

~DA35-36

Integrating Differences within Ourselves

"Man has many functions or rather he is the interplay of many functions. The child grows to manhood through interpenetrating – with his family, at school, at work, with his play group, with his art group: the carpenter may join the Arts and Crafts to find there an actualization of spirit for which he is fitted, and so on and so on. All the different sides of our nature develop by the process of compounding. If you shut a man up in his occupation, you refuse him the opportunity of full growth. The task has been given to humanity to 'Know thyself,' but man cannot know himself without knowing the many sides of his self. His essential self is the possibility of the multiple expression of spirit."
~NS288

Integrating Differences within Ourselves

"The man who knows the 'best' society of Petrograd, Paris, London and New York, and that only, is a narrow man because the ideals and standards of the 'best' society of London, Paris and New York are the same. He knows life across but not down – it is a horizontal civilization instead of a vertical one, with all the lack of depth and height of everything horizontal. This man has always been among the same kind of people, his life has not been enlarged and enriched by the friction of ideas and ideals which comes from the meeting of people of different opportunities and different tastes and different standards."

~NS195-196

"Individuality is the capacity for union. The measure of individuality is the depth and breadth of true relation. I am an individual not as far as I am apart from, but as far as I am a part of other men. Evil is non-relation."
~NS62

1 THE DIFFERENCE OF EVERY MOMENT

"Education therefore is not chiefly to teach children a mass of things which have been true up to the present moment; moreover it is not to teach them to learn about life as fast as it is made, not even to interpret life, but above and beyond everything, to create life for themselves. Hence education should be largely the training in making choices. The aim of all proper training is not rigid adherence to a crystallized right (since in ethics, economics or politics there is no crystallized right), but the power to make a new choice at every moment."
~NS54

The Difference of Every Moment

"To be experience-conscious is to know the difference between one moment and another – the beginning of all aesthetic appreciation. Barrett Wendell used to tell us that if we should stand on the Harvard bridge today at the same hour as yesterday and look at exactly the same sunset, if that were possible, still it would not be the same experience as yesterday because we should be different – we should be one day older. No experience can ever be repeated, and in this fact we find all the tragedy of life and at the same time its glory – its irrepressible movement. The knowledge of this fundamental principle I think every teacher should bring to his students."

~TS6

"Our safeguard against crystallization is that every fresh unity means the throwing out of myriad fresh differences – our safeguard is that the universe knows no static unity. Unification means sterilization; unifying means a perpetual generating."
~NS287

The Difference of Every Moment

"Unity is always a process, not a product."
~DA19

The Difference of Every Moment

"And the greatest lesson of all is to know that every moment is new."
~NS54

The Difference of Every Moment

"My response is not to a crystallized product of the past, static for the moment of meeting; while I am behaving, the environment is changing because of my behaving, and my behavior is a response to the new situation which I, in part, have created."
~CE63-64

The Difference of Every Moment

"The surge of life sweeps through the given similarity, the common ground, and breaks it up into a thousand differences. This tumultuous, irresistible flow of life is our existence: the unity, the common, is but for an instant, it flows on to new differings which adjust themselves anew in fuller, more varied, richer synthesis. The moment when similarity achieves itself as a composite of working, seething forces, it throws out its myriad new differings. The torrent flows into a pool, works, ferments, and then rushes forth until all is again gathered into the new pool of its own unifying. This is the process of evolution."

~NS35

1 Differences Make the World Go Round

"There is not room on this planet for a lot of similar nations, but only for a lot of different nations. A group of nations must create a group culture which shall be broader than the culture of one nation alone. There must be a world-ideal, a whole-civilization, in which the ideals and the civilization of every nation can find a place."
~NS345-346

"It is said that a mighty struggle is before us by-and-by when East meets West, and in that shock will be decided which of these civilizations shall rule the world – that this is to be the great world-decision. No, the great world-decision is that each nation needs equally every other, therefore each will not only protect, but foster and increase the other that thereby it may increase its own stature."

~NS446

"We must indeed, as the extreme militarists tell us, 'wipe out' our enemies, but we do not wipe out our enemies by crushing them. The old-fashioned hero went out to conquer his enemy; the modern hero goes out to disarm his enemy through creating a mutual understanding."
~NS345

"If the Allies win, Germany should not be punished by keeping her out of a European league; she must be shown how to take her place within it. And it must be remembered that we do not join a league of nations solely to work out our relations to one another, but to learn to work for the larger whole, for international values. Until this lesson is learned no league of nations can be successful."
~NS353

"In making a plea for some experiment in international cooperation I remember, with humiliation, that we have fought because it is the easy way. Fighting solves no problems. The problems which brought on this war will all be there to be settled when the war ends. But we have war as the line of least resistance. We have war when the mind gives up its job of agreeing as too difficult. It is often stated that conflict is a necessity of the human soul, and that if conflict should ever disappear from among us, individuals would deteriorate and society collapse. But the effort of agreeing is so much more strenuous than the comparatively easy stunt of fighting that we can harden our spiritual muscles much more effectively on the former than the latter."
~NS356-357

Differences Make the World Go Round

"From war to peace is not from the strenuous to the easy existence; it is from the futile to the effective, from the stagnant to the active, from the destructive to the creative way of life."
~NS357-358

"But why should we be more efficiently organized for war than for peace? Is our proverbial carelessness to be pricked into effectiveness only by emergency calls? Is the only motive you can offer us for efficiency – to win? Or, if that is an instinctive desire, can we not change the goal to be as eager to win other things as war?"

~NS248-249

"If the essential characteristic of war is doing things together, let us begin to do things together in Peace. Yet not an artificial doing things together, we could so easily fall into that, but an entire reorganization of life so that the doing things together shall be the natural way – the way we shall all want to do things."
~NS195

2

Mary Parker Follett on Group Organization

We live in a world full of paradoxes. Information and communication technologies seem to make possible new forms of interactions between human beings, yet humanity seems to keep struggling with the challenge of "living together".

According to Mary Parker Follett, group experience is at the heart of learning "living together". For her, the group process is the one that both expresses individual differences and integrates them into unity. Specifically, the group process consists of reciprocal influences that contribute to create a collective idea and, at the same time, fully reveal the individual, renewed through the group.

Finally, the group process is the basis of democracy, considered as a system that promotes the exchange of ideas and the creation of collective solutions.

Follett's knowledge about such issues as group dynamics, leadership and democracy is rooted in her own experience as a social entrepreneur in Boston before writing *The New State* in 1918. From 1900, she initiated or was involved in the management of several large size public projects; she helped develop access to education and community activities through the implementation of Community Centers around the city of Boston.

Following are six subcategories of quotes that highlight Mary Parker Follett's perspective on group organization.

1. Group organization as a new method

This first selection of quotes shows how much group organization is a breakthrough method from conventional top-down political tendencies. Follett wrote a lot about the "newness" of her era; focusing on learning attitudes and behaviors for human cooperation was very "new".

2. Group process is a creative process

When group members meet and confront ideas through the group process, ideas are not just transformed. With the group process, new ideas emerge.

3. Group organization vs. crowd organization

Follett helps us distinguish group organization from crowd organization. Crowd organization has to do with imitation, suggestion and mass behavior. Group organization has to do with innovation and creative behavior.

4. The group, the leader and power

The leader is not outside the group but integrates the group process and develops group power. The leader is powerful as he or she makes the group powerful.

5. Group organization as a practice

This section offers practical examples of group organization through notions such as *experience meetings* and *neighborhood groups*.

6. The Technique of Democracy is Group Organization

The group process by which the collective idea is created involves what Follett calls circular behavior (see also Integration section). The majority rule idea of traditional democratic systems denies this. Follett suggests group organizing as the method for democratic living.

2 Group Organization as a New Method

"Group organization will create the new world we are now blindly feeling after, for creative force comes from the group, creative power is evolved through the activity of the group life."
~NS3

"The group organization movement means the substitution of intention for accident, of organized purpose for scattered desire. It rests on the solid assumption that this is a man-made not a machine-made world, that men and women are capable of constructing their own life, and that not upon socialism or any rule or any order or any plan or any utopia can we rest our hearts, but only on the force of a united and creative citizenship."

~NS8

"The potentialities of the individual remain potentialities until they are released by group life. Man discovers his true nature, gains his true freedom only through the group. Group organization must be the new method of politics because the modes by which the individual can be brought forth and made effective are the modes of practical politics.

But who is the individual we have been seeking, who is the individual we are to find within the group? Certainly not the particularist individual. Every man to count as one? That was once our slogan. Now we have relegated it to a mechanical age. Today we see that every man must count for infinitely more than one because he is not part of a whole, a cog in a machine, not even an organ in an organism, but from one point of view the whole itself."
~NS6

2 GROUP PROCESS IS A CREATIVE PROCESS

Group Process is a Creative Process

"Whenever we have a real group something new is actually created. We can now see therefore that the object of group life is not to find the best individual thought, but the collective thought. A committee meeting isn't like a prize show aimed at calling out the best each can possibly produce and then the prize (the vote) awarded to the best of all these individual opinions. The object of a conference is not to get at a lot of different ideas, as is often thought, but just the opposite – to get at one idea. There is nothing rigid or fixed about thoughts, they are entirely plastic, and ready to yield themselves completely to their master – the group spirit."
~NS30

Group Process is a Creative Process

"The object of a committee meeting is first of all to create a common idea. I do not go to a committee meeting merely to give my own ideas. If that were all, I might write my fellow-members a letter. But neither do I go to learn other people's ideas. If that were all, I might ask each to write me a letter. I go to a committee meeting in order that all together we may create a group idea, an idea which will be better than any one of our ideas alone, moreover which will be better than all of our ideas added together. For this group idea will not be produced by any process of addition, but by the interpenetration of us all. This subtle psychic process by which the resulting idea shapes itself is the process we want to study."

~NS24

Group Process is a Creative Process

"Thus the majority idea is not the group idea. Suppose I belong to a committee composed of five: of A, B, C, D and myself. According to the old theory of my duties as a committee member I might say, 'A agrees with me, if I can get B to agree with me that will make a majority and I can carry my point.' That is, we five can then present this idea to the world as our group idea. But this is not a group idea, although it may be the best substitute we can get for the moment. To a genuine group idea every man must contribute what is in him to contribute. Thus even the passing of a unanimous vote by a group of five does not prove the existence of a group idea if two or three (or even one) out of indifference or laziness or prejudice, or shut-upness, or a misconception of their function, have not added their individual thought to the creation of the group thought. No member of a group which is to create can be passive. All must be active and constructively active."
~NS27-28

"Let us consider what is required of the individual in order that the group idea shall be produced. First and foremost each is to do his part. But just here we have to get rid of some rather antiquated notions. The individual is not to facilitate agreement by courteously waiving his own point of view. That is just a way of shirking. Nor may I say, 'Others are able to plan this better than I.' Such an attitude is the result either of laziness or of a misconception. There are probably many present at the conference who could make wiser plans than I alone, but that is not the point, we have come together each to give something. I must not subordinate myself, I must affirm myself and give my full positive value to that meeting. And as the psychic coherence of the group can be obtained only by the full contribution of every member, so we see that a readiness to compromise must be no part of the individual's attitude."
~NS26

Group Process is a Creative Process

"What I have tried to show in this book is that the social process may be conceived either as the opposing and battle of desires with the victory of one over the other, or as the confronting and integrating of desires. The former means non-freedom for both sides, the defeated bound to the victor, the victor bound to the false situation thus created both bound. The latter means a freeing for both sides and increased total power or increased capacity in the world."
~CE301-302

"To free the energies of the human spirit is the high potentiality of all human association"
~CE303

Group Process is a Creative Process

"From the group process arise social understanding and true sympathy. At the same moment appears the social will which is the creative will. Many writers are laying stress on the *possibilities* of the collective will; what I wish to emphasize is the necessity of *creating* the collective will. Many people talk as if the collective will were lying round loose to be caught up whenever we like, but the fact is we must go to our group and see that it is brought into existence."

~NS48

Group Process is a Creative Process

"What then is the essence of the group process by which are evolved the collective thought and the collective wills? It is an acting and reacting, a single and identical process which brings out differences and integrates them into a unity. The complex reciprocal action, the intricate interweavings of the members of the group, is the social process."

~NS33

"The members of a group are reciprocally conditioning forces none of which acts as it would act if any one member were different or absent. You can often see this in a board of directors: if one director leaves the room, every man becomes slightly different."
~NS31

Group Process is a Creative Process

"We see now that the process of the many becoming one is not a metaphysical or mystical idea; psychological analysis shows us how we can at the same moment be the self and the other, it shows how we can be forever apart and forever united. It is by the group process that the transfiguration of the external into the spiritual takes place, that is, that what seems a series becomes a whole."

~NS33

2 Group Organization vs. Crowd Organization

Group Organization vs. Crowd Organization

"I have used group in this book with the meaning of men associating under the law of interpenetration as opposed to the law of the crowd – suggestion and imitation. This may be considered an arbitrary definition, but of course I do not care about the names, I only want to emphasize the fact that men meet under two different sets of laws. Social psychology may include both group psychology and crowd psychology, but of these two, group psychology is much the more important. For a good many years now we have been dominated by the crowd school, by the school which taught that people met together are governed by suggestion and imitation, and less notice has been taken of all the interplay which is the real social process that we have in a group but not in a crowd."
~NS22-23

Group Organization vs. Crowd Organization

"Suggestion is the law of the crowd, interpenetration of the group. When we study a crowd we see how quickly B takes A's ideas and also C and D and E; when we study a group we see that the ideas of A often arouse in B exactly opposite ones. Moreover, the crowd often deadens thought because it wants immediate action, which means an unthinking unanimity not a genuine collective thought. The group on the other hand stimulates thought. There are no "differences" in the crowd mind. Each person is swept away and does not stop to find out his own difference. In crowds we have unison, in groups harmony. We want the single voice but not the single note; that is the secret of the group. The enthusiasm and unanimity of a mass-meeting may warm an inexperienced heart, but the experienced know that this unanimity is largely superficial and is based on the spread of similar ideas, not the unifying of differences. A crowd does not distinguish between fervor and wisdom; a group usually does."
~NS86

Group Organization vs. Crowd Organization

"When we hear it stated as a commonplace of human affairs that combined action is less intelligent than individual action, we must point out that it all depends upon whether it is a crowd combination or a group combination."
~NS150

"The strength of the group does not depend on the greatest number of strong men, but on the strength of the bond between them, that is, on the amount of solidarity, on the best organization."
~NS96

Group Organization vs. Crowd Organization

"… The developed man is the group man and the group man neither accepts nor rejects, but joins his own thought with that of all he reads to make new thought. The group man is never sterile, he always brings forth."
~NS154

"And as the psychic coherence of the group can be obtained only by the full contribution of every member, so we see that a readiness to compromise must be no part of the individual's attitude."
~NS26

"An English writer says that we get leadership from the fact that men are capable of being moved to such service by the feeling of altruism; he attributes public spirit to love, pity, compassion and sensitiveness to suffering. This is no doubt largely true at the present moment, but public spirit will sometime mean, as it does today in many instances, the recognition that it is not merely that my city, my nation needs me, but that I need it as the larger sphere of a larger self-expression."

~NS83

Group Organization vs. Crowd Organization

"This individual has belonged to many other groups, has discussed with many men, or even if he has lived his life apart he has read newspapers and magazines, books and letters, and has mingled his ideas with those he has found there. Thus the 'individual' idea he brings to a group is not really an 'individual' idea; it is the result of the process of interpenetration, but by bringing it to a new group and soaking it in that the interpenetration becomes more complex."

~NS94

Group Organization vs. Crowd Organization

"I have spoken of the psychological tendency for group to seek group. Moreover, it is not possible to isolate yourself in your local group because few local needs can be met without joining with other localities, which have these same needs, in order to secure city or state action…

And we join not only to secure city and state but also federal action. If we want a river or harbor appropriation, we go to Congress… And we do not stop even at Washington…

And then we have learned to be truly citizens of Boston, we must discover how Boston and other cities, how cities and the rural communities can join. And so on and so on. We are pragmatists because we do not want to unite with the state imaginatively, we want to be the state; we want to actualize and feel our way every moment, let every group open the way for a larger group, let every circumference become the center of a new circumference. My neighborhood group opens the path to the State."

~NS251-254

Group Organization vs. Crowd Organization

"The individual not the group must be the basis of organization. But the individual is created by many groups, his vote cannot express his relation to one group; it must ideally, I have said, express the whole from his point of view, actually it must express as much of the whole as the variety of his group life makes possible."
~NS180

Group Organization vs. Crowd Organization

"A workman said to me, 'I have sometimes felt in a conference committee a double responsibility, a responsibility to both sides.' Such a feeling is the beginning of a consciousness of unity, and when you get a consciousness of unity, self-interest is a good thing, for then it means the interest of the group with which you have identified yourself....

A man expands as his will expands. A man's individuality stops where his power of collective willing stops. If he cannot will beyond his trade union then we must write upon his tombstone 'This was a union man'. If he cannot will beyond his church, then he is a church man. The soul of the process is always the individual, but the individual forever escapes the form."
~DA216

2 THE GROUP, THE LEADER AND POWER

"We must also consider how far groups are power organizations. For example, the trade unions' demand for higher wages is the demand (desire) of individuals, not of a group; they join in order to put power back of the demand. There is no group 'instinct'. My loyalty to my group is stimulated when I need the power of the group to satisfy needs; my loyalty to my trade union is stimulated when my children have no shoes."

~CE183

"The leader guides the group and is at the same time himself guided by the group, is always a part of the group. No one can truly lead except from within. One danger of conceiving the leader as outside is that then what ought to be group loyalty will become personal loyalty. When we have a leader within the group these two loyalties can merge."
~NS229

"We should think not only of what the leader does to the group, but also of what the group does to the leader...

He must know how to create a group power rather than to express a personal power. He must make the team."

~DA248

"I believe we shall soon think of the leader as one who can organize the experience of the group, make it all available and most effectively available, and thus get the full power of the group. It is by organizing experience that we transform experience into power. And that is what experience is for, to be made into power."
~DA258

2 GROUP ORGANIZATION AS A PRACTICE

"There is no such thing as a neighborhood in its true sense, something more, that is, than the physical contiguity of people, until you have a neighborhood consciousness. Rows of houses, rows of streets, do not make a neighborhood. The place bond must give way to a consciousness of real union.
This neighborhood consciousness can be evolved in five ways:
1. By regular meetings of neighbors for the consideration of neighborhood and civic problems, not merely sporadic and occasional meetings for specific objects.
2. By a genuine discussion at these regular meetings.
3. By learning together – through lectures, classes, clubs; by sharing one another's experience through social intercourse; by learning forms of community art expression; in short by leading an actual community life.
4. By taking more and more responsibility for the life of the neighborhood.
5. By establishing some regular connection between the neighborhood and city, state and national governments."
~NS204

Group Organization as a Practice

"I should like, for instance, to try experience meetings. The first step in these would be to present the subject under consideration in such a way as to show clearly its relation to all our daily lives. This is very important and usually neglected; I have never heard anyone tell people the actual difference in their own lives a League of Nations might make. The second step would be for each one of us to try to find in our own experience anything that would throw light on the question. I am hoping that this might prove sufficiently interesting to induce us to put up with the 'accurate information.' Also that after such meetings have become a part of our community life, we should begin to observe and analyze our experience much more carefully than we do at present; it is almost wholly insignificant to us now as having social value. And I am hoping much more than this: that we shall take an experimental attitude toward our experience, and have many experiments to report with reasons for their success or failure, and suggestions as to what direction new experiments should take. The third step would be to see if we could unite our various experiences, one with the other and with the material provided by the expert. The material of the expert would always thus be thrown into the situation, not put up for acceptance or rejection."
~CE212-213

2 The Technique of Democracy is Group Organization

*The Technique of Democracy
is Group Organization*

"Formerly the supporters of democracy, concerned with the machinery of government, aimed to find those forms which should give voice to 'the people,' but for some time now we have not given much thought to this consideration: the thinkers certainly have not, and the community centre movement, the workmen's education movement, the cooperative movement, to mention only two or three, are not based on the assumption that the will of the people is 'instinctively' good, and that our institutions exist merely to get at this will, to give it voice, etc. The essential aim of these, the most democratic movements we have, is to train ourselves, to learn how to use the work of experts, to find our will, to educate our will, to integrate our wills."

~CE6

*The Technique of Democracy
is Group Organization*

"Thus group organization releases us from the domination of mere numbers. Thus democracy transcends time and space, it can never be understood except as a spiritual force. Majority rule rests on numbers; democracy rests on the well-grounded assumption that society is neither a collection of units nor an organism but a network of human relations. Democracy is not worked out at the polling-booths; it is the bringing forth of a genuine collective will, one to which every single being must contribute the whole of his complex life, as one which every single being must express the whole of at one point. Thus the essence of democracy is creating. The technique of democracy is group organization. Many men despise politics because they see that politics manipulate, but make nothing. If politics are to be the highest activity of man, as they should be, they must be clearly understood as creative."
~NS7

*The Technique of Democracy
is Group Organization*

"The fundamental reason for the study of group psychology is that no one can give us democracy, we must learn democracy. To be a democrat is not to decide on a certain form of human association, it is to learn how to live with other men."
~NS22

*The Technique of Democracy
is Group Organization*

"The chief need of society to-day is an enlightened, progressive and organized public opinion, and the first step towards an enlightened and organized public opinion is an enlightened and organized group opinion. When public opinion becomes conscious of itself it will have a justified confidence in itself. Then the 'people,' born of an associated life, will truly govern."
~NS226

3

Mary Parker Follett on the Process of Integration

Follett's perspective on integration, at its core, is a process for the constructive and creative use of dynamic interaction. It builds on differences – or to use another term, conflict – to create new dynamics and development. Simply put, integration is like taking two different things, putting them together, and creating something entirely new.

Follett's idea of integration is in no way meant to resemble compromise. In fact, she deplores compromise, a position that set her at odds with the mainstream thinking of her time – and still does today. For Follett, to compromise means to sacrifice. This is why conflict handled through compromise will often resurface, because we stop short of truly understanding each other and what this conflict means to us.

An essential element of integrative behavior is the notion of power-with (see also Leadership section): a joint approach to power that provides space for joint fact-finding, joint interpretations and joint action. It forms the foundation of Follett's vision of leadership and democracy.

Humans are complex beings living in complex diverse societies. Specialists see very clearly through the lens of their specialty, but if we are to solve complex human problems, we must learn to see the panorama and integrate the different points of view. Follett's ideas shows us ways to do this.

In this chapter, we introduce the concept of integration through six sub-themes:

1. The creative intelligence of integration

Differences hold the potential to disintegrate or integrate. Integration allows us to harness individual and group differences into a creative process.

2. Constructive conflict through integration

Integration is at the heart of social development and creative conflict resolution. As individuals or in groups, to grow, we must learn; to learn we must examine; to examine, we must engage.

3. Integration goes beyond compromise

Compromise is based on two flawed premises: that everyone wants the same thing, and that this "thing" is in short supply.

4. Integration and the circular response

Follett demonstrates that we are constantly involved in dynamic interaction with others and with our environment. This dynamic interaction generates friction, highlights our differences and challenges us to grow.

5. Living integration

Through the process of integration (that is, to identify, deconstruct, reflect, and to collaboratively reconstruct) one can come into contact with the uniqueness of our needs and the myriad of ways to reach fulfillment. Most importantly, the individual is not lost in the process because one's needs and goals are accounted for throughout and bolstered through individual engagement.

6. Experiencing power and democracy though integration

Follett explains that integration is an essential aspect of democratic living: developing a unity of vision and action while maintaining the integrity of the individual. Integration allows for co-creation of power and sustainable decision-making.

3 THE CREATIVE INTELLIGENCE OF INTEGRATION

The Creative Intelligence of Integration

"Integration, the most suggestive word of contemporary psychology, is, I believe, the active principle of human intercourse scientifically lived. When differing interests meet, they need not oppose but only confront each other. The confronting of interests may result in either one of four things: (1) voluntary submission of one side; (2) struggle and the victory of one side over the other; (3) compromise; or (4) integration. Enough has been said of domination whether obtained by show of power or use of power; unless we can learn some other process than that we shall always be controlled by those who can summon to themselves the greatest force of the moment, militarist, economic, or whatever it may be. As one nation gains power, others, to that extent, come under its domination. As trade unions gain power, they use it against the rest of the community; and the effect of this is merely that other groups wait to gather force for their moment."

~CE156

The Creative Intelligence of Integration

"Suppose I disagree with you in a discussion and we make no effort to join our ideas, but 'fight it out.' I hammer away with my idea, I try to find all the weakest parts of yours, I refuse to see anything good in what you think. That is not nearly so difficult as trying to recognize all the possible subtle interweavings of thought, how one part of your thought, or even one aspect of one part, may unite with one part or one aspect of one part of mine, etc. Likewise with cooperation and competition in business: cooperation is going to prove so much more difficult than competition that there is not the slightest danger of any one getting soft under it."

~NS357

"To accept the philosophy of integration is to change somewhat our ideas of sacrifice, so long held by many. I put domination and sacrifice together as based on the same error. If I dominate you, *I* get what I want. If I sacrifice myself to you, you get what *you* want. I do not see why one way is any better than the other. The only gain would be if we could both have what we want."

~DA215

The Creative Intelligence of Integration

"There is only one test for the value of wants: their confronting or conflict, but conflict constructively conceived, not as resulting necessarily in adjustment, mere adjustment, but as opening the way for integrating."
~CE260

The Creative Intelligence of Integration

"All diversity wisely handled may lead to the 'something new' but if one submits to the other, or a compromise is made, we have no progress. Each must persist until a way is found by which neither is absorbed but by which both can contribute to the solution."
~CE162

The Creative Intelligence of Integration

"Another mediator expressed what I think is essentially the same idea in this way: 'The two parties come together. There comes a moment in the negotiations when a new relationship between them is born. I am the midwife to that birth.'"

~DA243

The Creative Intelligence of Integration

"Thus when we integrate there is nothing left to pigeon-hole. Our great judges are those who do not pigeon-hole but integrate. It is the difference between a mechanical and a creating intelligence. Those who interpret mechanically are 'robots.' The 'robots,' made in factories to do a man's work for him, had mechanical intelligence; then could have taken experience and put it into pigeon-holes, then when they needed principle or precedent they could have gone to the pigeon-holes and take out what 'corresponded.' But men who are exercising that kind of intelligence are not claiming their birth-right; what man is capable of is activity that creates."

~CE137

The Creative Intelligence of Integration

"I have said that on the biological level, growth is by integration, by the continuous integration of simple, specific responses. I have said that we see the same law in operation on the personal level; diverse tendencies are united into new action patterns. I have said that in the case of two individuals, that is, on the social level, here, too, we get control through effective integration. Authority should arise within the unifying process. As every living process is subject to its own authority, that is, the authority evolved by or involved in the process itself, so social control is generated by the process itself or rather, the activity of self-creating coherence is the controlling activity."
~DA204

The Creative Intelligence of Integration

"We must put everything we can into each fresh experience, but we shall not get the same things out which we put in if it is a fruitful experience, if it is part of our progressing life… We have the choice with each fresh experience, if we do not disregard it altogether, of either pigeon-holing it to take out at some future time when a similar circumstance arises (a similar circumstance never will arise), or of integrating it with all the rest of our experience. We integrate our experience, and then the richer human being that we are goes into the new experience; again we give ourself and always by the giving rise above the old self."
~CE136-137

3 Constructive Conflict through Integration

Constructive Conflict through Integration

"We need a technique for human relations based on the preservation of the integrity of the individual. Of late years we have heard too much of the collective life as an aim in itself. But who cares for the 'collective life.' It is usually a shibboleth of empty words. What we care about is the productive life, and the first test of *productive* power of collective life is its nourishment of the individual. The second test is whether the contributions of individuals can be fruitfully united."

~CExiii

Constructive Conflict through Integration

"Social conflict is constructive when it follows this normal process, when the release of energy is by one and the same movement carrying itself to a higher level. What I have tried to show in this book is that the social process may be conceived either as the opposing and battling of desires with the victory of one over the other, or as the confronting and integrating of desires. The former means non-freedom for both sides, the defeated bound to the victor, the victor bound to the false situation thus created – both bound. The latter means a freeing for both sides and increased total power or increased capacity in the world. The core of the development, expansion, growth, progress of humanity is the confronting and gripping of opposites. Integration is both the keel and the rudder of life: it supports all life's structures and guides every activity.

This thought must be ever before us in social research. For we believe in the inexhaustible resources of life, in the fresh powers constantly springing up.

The test of the vitality of any experience is its power to unite into a living, generating activity its self-yielding differences. We seek a richly diversified experience where every difference strengthens and reinforces the other… The activity of co-creating is the core of democracy, the essence of citizenship, the condition of world-citizenship."
~CE301-302

"Here we should have not necessarily the opposing, but the confronting, of interests. This confronting would make apparent many incompatibilities of interests, but does not judge the case beforehand as to what shall be done about it. Confront does not mean combat. In other words, it leaves the possibility of integrating as the method of the meeting of difference."

~CE120

3 Integration Goes Beyond Compromise

Integration Goes Beyond Compromise

"Integration might be considered a qualitative adjustment, compromise a quantitative one. In the former there is a change in the ideas and their action tendencies; in the latter there is mere barter of opposed 'rights of way'... In compromise, I say, there is no qualitative changes in our thinking. Partisanship starves our nature: I am so intent on my own values that other values have got starved out of me; this represents a loss in my nature, in the whole of my personality. Through an interpenetrating of understanding, the quality of one's own thinking is changed; we are sensitized to an appreciation of other values. By not interpenetrating, by simply lining up values and conceding some for the sake of getting the agreement necessary for action, our thinking stays just where it was. In integration all the overtones of value are utilized."

~CE163

"One advantage of integration over compromise I have not yet mentioned. If we get only compromise, the conflict will come up again and again in some other form, for in compromise we give up part of our desire, and because we shall not be content to rest there, sometime we shall try to get the whole of our desire. Watch industrial controversy, watch international controversy, and see how often this occurs. Only integration really stabilizes. But by stabilization I do not mean anything stationary. Nothing ever stays put. I mean only that that particular conflict is settled and the next occurs on a higher level."

~DA35

"Moreover, the doctrine of integrating interests does away with that of the balance of interests which has so many advocates… In fact, observation of industrial controversy for the last ten years leads me to think that those disputes which are 'settled' merely by the balance of power are not really settled at all. The slightest shift of power brings the matter up again with accumulated rancor and hard feeling. The balance theory gets us nowhere in law or politics or international relations."

~CE45

3 Living Integration

"Life is not a movie for us; you can never watch life because you are always in life… Does this make an impasse for us? On the contrary, the evolving situation, the "progressive integrations", the ceaseless interweaving of new specific respondings, is the whole forward movement of existence; there is no adventure for those who stand at the counters of life and match samples."
~CE13

"Integration of activities usually outruns integration of ideas. We have all of us noticed this in conference where we see ourselves and fellows influenced both by the situation as it was when we entered the conference, and also as it has developed during the conference. This means that the life processes integrate faster than our minds can integrate them."
~CE176

"… Integration, the resolution of conflict, the harmonizing of difference, must take place on the motor level, not on the intellectual level. We cannot get genuine agreement by mere discussion in conference. As our responses are governed by past habits, by what has been incorporated in the organism, the only way of getting other responses is by getting other things incorporated in the organism… Genuine integration occurs in the sphere of activities, and not of ideas or wills."

~CE150

Living Integration

"I have said that our main consideration is always with the integration of activities. It is thus impossible to speak of the integration of persons. An individual as an abstraction does not meet another individual as an abstraction; it is always activity meeting activity... What happens when I meet another person for the first time? He comes to me always pushing in front of him his picture of himself; as I get to know him, do I see that picture gradually disappear, leaving his real self? Not at all, I put my own interpretative picture in its place. Where, then, is the real person – for me? It is in his behaving (and his account of his behaving is part of his behavior) plus my interpretation of his behavior as shown by my behaving."
~CE177

"We should not try to create the attitude we want, although that is the usual phrase, but the attitude required for cooperative study and decision."
~DA61

Living Integration

"The first rule, then, for obtaining integration is to put your cards on the table, face the real issue, uncover the conflict, and bring the whole thing into the open."
~DA38

"The most familiar example of integrating as the social process is when two or three people meet to decide on some course of action, and separate with a purpose, a will, which was not possessed by anyone when he came to the meeting but is the result of the interweaving of all. In this true social process there takes place neither absorption nor compromise."
~CP1

Living Integration

"Not all difference, however, can be integrated. That we must face fully, but it is certain that there are fewer irreconcilable activities than we at present think, although it often takes ingenuity, a 'creative intelligence' to find the integration."

~CE163

Living Integration

"... Let us consider the chief *obstacles to integration*. It requires a high order of intelligence, keen perception and discrimination, more than all, a brilliant inventiveness.

... Another obstacle to integration is that our way of life has habituated many of us to enjoy domination. Integration seems to many a tamer affair; it leaves no 'thrills' of conquest...

Another obstacle to integration is that the matter in dispute is often theorized over instead of being taken up as a proposed activity...

A serious obstacle to integration which every business man should consider is the language used. We have noted the necessity of making preparation in the other man, and in ourselves too, for the attitude most favorable to reconciliation...

Finally, perhaps the greatest of all obstacles to integration is our lack of training for it."
~DA45-48

Living Integration

"In my emphasis on integration, it must not be supposed, however, that I ignore the part of disintegration in the creative process… Yet however often it is disruption which leads to fresh and more fruitful unitings, however often it is the salutary means by which formal wholes give place to functional unities, yet disruption is only a part of that total life process to which, in its more comprehensive aspect, we may give the name integration."

~CE178

Living Integration

"You will notice that to break up a problem into its various parts involves the *examination of symbols,* involves, that is, the careful scrutiny of the language used to see what it really means. A friend of mine wanted to go to Europe, but also she did not want to spend the money it would cost. Was there any integration? Yes, she found one. In order to understand it, let us use the method I am advocating; let us ask, what did 'going to Europe' symbolize to her? In order to do that, we have to break up this whole, 'going to Europe.' What does 'going to Europe' stand for to different people? A sea voyage, seeing beautiful places, meeting new people, a rest or change from daily duties, and a dozen other things. Now, this woman had taught for a few years after leaving college and then had gone away and led a somewhat secluded life for a good many years. 'Going to Europe' was to her a symbol, not of snow mountains, or cathedrals, or pictures, but of meeting people – that was what she wanted. When she was asked to teach in a summer school of young men and women where she would meet a rather interesting staff of teachers and a rather interesting group of students, she immediately accepted. This was her integration. This was not a substitution for her wish, it was her *real* wish fulfilled."

~DA41-42

3 Integration and the Circular Response

Integration and the Circular Response

"In human relations, as I have said, this is obvious: I never react to you but to you-plus-me; or to be more accurate, it is I-plus-you reacting to you-plus-me. 'I' can never influence 'you' because you have already influenced me; that is, in the very process of meeting, by the very process of meeting, we both become something different. It begins even before we meet, in the anticipation of meeting."
~CE62-63

"A good example of circular response is a game of tennis. A serves. The way B returns the ball depends partly on the way it was served to him. A's next play will depend on his own original serve plus the return of B, and so on and so on. We see this in discussion. We see this in most activity between one and another. Mischievous or idle boys say, 'Let's start something'; we must remember that whenever we act we have always 'started something', behavior precipitates behavior in others."

~DA43

"Circular behavior as the basis of integration gives us the key to constructive conflict."
~DA45

Integration and the Circular Response

"This 'total situation' is often looked at as a total picture; it is thought that you can get all the factors if you examine the picture in sufficient detail. But a total situation is never a total picture; it is a total activity in which the activity of individual and activity of environment constantly interweave. What the social worker tries to do is to bring about the *kind* of interweaving from which it follows that further responses from environment, further responses from individual, will mean a *progressive* experience."
~CE105-6

3 Experiencing Power and Democracy through Integration

Experiencing Power and Democracy through Integration

"What is the central problem of social relations? It is the question of power; this is the problem of industry, of politics, of international affairs. But our task is not to learn where to place power; it is how to develop power. We frequently hear nowadays of 'transferring' power as the panacea for our ills. Transfer power to occupational groups, we are told, and all will be well; but the transference of power has been the whole course of history – power passing to priests or kings or barons, to council or soviet. Are we satisfied to continue this puss-in-the-corner game? We shall certainly do so as long as we think that the transference of power is the way of progress. Genuine power can only be grown, it will slip from the every arbitrary hand that grasps it; for genuine power is not coercive control, but coactive control. Coercive power is the curse of the universe; coactive power, the enrichment and advancement of every human soul."

~CExii-xiii

Experiencing Power and Democracy through Integration

"The subject of power needs, I have said, much empirical study, but at present the greatest light on the subject is, I think, that given by the psychological principle of integration. The integrating of wants precludes the necessity of gaining power to satisfy desire. In the library today, in one of the smaller rooms, someone wanted the window open, I wanted it shut. We opened the window in the next room where no one was sitting. This was not a compromise because there was no lopping off of desire; we both got what we really wanted. For I did not want a closed room, I simply did not want the north wind to blow directly on me; likewise the other occupant did not want that particular window open, he simply wanted more air in the room. Therefore, by the process... – breaking-up wholes, finding out what we really wanted – an integration was possible without resorting to power. By reducing the area of irreconcilable controversy, you can reduce the area of arbitrary power."

~CE184-185

Experiencing Power and Democracy through Integration

"This kind of power, power-with, is what democracy should mean in politics or industry, but as we have not taken the means to get a genuine power, pseudo power has leapt into the saddle."
~CE187

Experiencing Power and Democracy through Integration

"The only possible way of getting rid of the greed and scramble of our present world is for all of us to realize that the power we are snatching at is not really power, not that which we are really seeking, that the way to gain genuine power, even that which we ourselves really want, is by an integrative process."
~CE188

Experiencing Power and Democracy through Integration

"The more power I have over myself the more capable I am of joining fruitfully with you and with you developing power in the new unit thus formed our two selves. The more power America has over herself the more capable she is of joining fruitfully with other nations and thus developing power in a new unit, a union of nations. Influence then in the wrong sense is when you choose to appeal to those tendencies which will help your purpose, not mine. Influence in a good sense is when you do not try to bind (me to you) but to free."

~ CE189-190

Experiencing Power and Democracy through Integration

"Any attempt at arbitrary control sets up antagonisms in the other person or group that will defeat you in the end."

~ CE190

Experiencing Power and Democracy through Integration

"The principle of integrating interests is not yet sufficiently recognized and acted on by jurists and economists, the principle of integrating *power* is not sufficiently acknowledged by political scientists. But while many political scientists and economists as well as statesmen and labor arbitrators have stuck to the theory of the balance of power, of the equilibrium of interests, yet life continually escapes them, for whenever we advance we slip from the bondage of equilibrium."
~CE53

Experiencing Power and Democracy through Integration

"I have said that on the biological level, growth is by integration, by the continuous integration of simple, specific responses. I have said that we see the same law in operation on the personal level; diverse tendencies are united into new action patterns. I have said that in the case of two individuals, that is, on the social level, here, too, we get control through effective integration. Authority should arise within the unifying process. As every living process is subject to its own authority, that is, the authority evolved by or involved in the process itself, so social control is generated by the process itself. Or rather, the activity of self-creating coherence is the controlling activity."

~DA204

Experiencing Power and Democracy through Integration

"The choice of war or peace is not the choice between effort and stagnation. We have thought of peace as the lambs lying down together after browsing on the consciousness of their happy agreements. We have thought of peace as a letting go and war as a girding up. We have thought of peace as the passive and war as the active way of living. The opposite is true. War is not the most strenuous life. It is a kind of rest-cure compared to the task of reconciling our differences. I knew a young business man who went to the Spanish war who said when he came back that it had been as good as going to a sanitarium; he had simply obeyed commands and had not made a decision or thought a thought since he left home."
~NS357-8

*Experiencing Power and Democracy
through Integration*

"Let us note, too, that if control arises within the unifying process, then the more highly integrated unity you have, the more self-direction you get. When bankers, manufacturers, workers, and consumers, learn how to form an integrative unity, then we shall have a large degree of social control."
~DA205

"We have the will of the people ideally when all desires are satisfied. In a power-society, however, it is the desire of the dominant classes which by the sorcery of consent becomes 'the will of the people'. The aim of democracy should be integrating-desires."
~CE209

4

Mary Parker Follett on Leadership

The prevailing leadership theory in Follett's time was The Great Man Theory. It stated that leaders were a rare heroic breed of individuals destined by their innate traits (e.g. charisma, intelligence, wisdom, or political skill) to lead. Followers on the other hand did not possess nor could they acquire these leadership traits.

While the notion of "leader" was generally understood as the one who had ascendancy and could have others follow his or her will, Follett proposed a more dynamic and integrative view. The leader's work for Follett was one of initiative yes, but most of all one of integrating all the various influences within a group into a unified and creative force. At the heart of her leadership philosophy was her proposition to move from a conventional *power-over* management model to what she called *power-with* management. The leader according to Follett has power *with* people, not *over* them. He or she has power *with* the situation, not *over* it. Another formulation she proposed was to move from *coercive power* to *coactive power*.

Although these collaborative and circular notions of power and leadership gained some recognition in her time, it is striking to see how contemporary or even *avant-garde* they still remain today. Mary Parker Follett remains a source of perennial wisdom on the subject of leadership. Following is a selection of texts which highlight her genius through eight themes:

1. Leadership as integrating

This first selection of quotes shows how Follett translates her core theme of integration within the concept of leadership. *Real power*, as she says, *comes from integration*.

2. Following the invisible leader

As Transformational Leadership Theory reminded us that leadership was more about following a common vision than about following a common person, Mary Parker Follett also presented leadership as the process of creating and following a common purpose, which she called *the invisible leader*.

3. Finding the law of the situation

Mary Parker Follett's perspective on scientific management is best exemplified by her suggestion to depersonalize the giving of orders and show that good decision-making in complex and changing environments involves the capacity to bring together different perspectives in order to then find and obey *the law of the situation.*

4. Leading is power-with

Although Follett recognizes that *power-over* cannot be eliminated, she indicates here the creative and life-enhancing force of a *power-with* posture and shows how integral it is to leadership. Leading is exercising power-with.

5. Empowering functional leadership

This section shows Mary Parker Follett's dynamic perspective on leadership. Beyond title and personality, Follett spoke of leadership based on functional competence. Leadership can be here, and it can be there too, depending on the competence needed in the situation.

6. Leading by example

The age-old wisdom that leaders lead first and foremost by example is also part of Follett's wisdom and beautifully presented in her boat anecdote in one of the selected quotes. The leader just did it!

7. Leaders develop leaders

This section shows again Follett's avant-garde humanism when we consider the cardinal importance for any leader today to recognize talent and develop people to become leaders themselves.

8. Leadership and collective creativity

Whether we speak of a business corporation or a community center, Follett saw all organizational settings as opportunities for individuals to join groups, create something valuable and become fuller individuals through the group experience. Leadership with that in mind becomes a creative force for personal and collective realization.

4 Leadership as Integrating

"The power of leadership is the power of integrating. This is the power which creates community. You can see it when two or three strangers or casual acquaintances are calling upon someone. With some hostesses you all talk across at one another as entirely separate individuals, pleasantly and friendlily, to be sure, but still across unbridged chasms; while other hostesses have the power of making you all feel for the moment related, as if you were one little community for the time being. This is a subtle as well as a valuable gift. It is one that leaders of men must possess. It is thus that the collective will is evolved from out the chaos of varied personality and complex circumstance."
~NS229

Leadership as Integrating

"This means that some people are beginning to conceive of the leader, not as the man in the group who is able to assert his individual will and get others to follow him, but as the one who knows how to relate these different wills so that they will have a driving force. He must know how to create a group power rather than to express a personal power. He must make the team. The power of leadership is the power of integrating. This is the power which creates community."

~DA248

"The leader is more responsible than anyone else for that integrative unity which is the aim of organization. As our business undertakings are not only becoming vast in size but also more complex in character, the success of these undertakings depends on their parts being so skillfully related one to another that they function effectively as a whole. The leader should be leader of a coherent group, of men who are finding their material welfare, their most effective expression, their spiritual satisfaction, through their relations to one another, through the functioning of the group to which they belong. If the old idea of leader was the man with compelling personality, the idea today is the man who is the expression of a harmonious and effective unity which he has helped to form and which he is able to make a going affair. We no longer think that the best leader is the greatest hustler or the most persuasive orator or even the best trader. The great leader is he who is able to integrate the experience of all and use it for a common purpose. All the ramifications of organization are the ways he does this; they are not set up to provide a machinery of following."
~DA267

Leadership as Integrating

"I have said that the leader must understand the situation, must see it as a whole, must see the inter-relation of all the parts. He must do more than this. He must see the evolving situation, the developing situation. His wisdom, his judgment, is used, not on a situation that is stationary, but on one that is changing all the time. The ablest administrators do not merely draw logical conclusions from the array of facts of the past which their expert assistants bring to them; they have a vision of the future. To be sure, business estimates are always, or should be, based on the probable future conditions. Sales policy, for instance, is guided not only by past sales but by probable future sales. The leader, however, must see all the future trends and unite them. Business is always developing. Decisions have to anticipate the development."
~DA263

"The most important thing to remember about unity is that there is no such thing. There is only unifying. You cannot get unity and expect it to last a day or five minutes. Every man in a business should be taking part in a certain process and that process is unifying. Every man's success in business depends largely, I believe, on whether he can learn something of this process, which is one neither of subordination nor of domination, but of each man learning to fit his work into that of every other in a spirit of co-operation, in an understanding of the methods of co-operation."
~FC51

Leadership as Integrating

"Business unifying must be understood as a process, not a product. We have to become process-conscious. I believe that is the first essential to the understanding of business organization. We sometimes hear the question discussed whether general policy should dictate departmental policies or departmental policies contribute to general policy. There is a deeper truth than either of these, and that is this something which I am trying to express to you namely, that it is the same activity which is making the whole and parts simultaneously. We never 'put parts together' even when we think we do. We watch parts behaving together, and the way they behave together is the whole. I say 'parts,' and people often speak of 'factors' or 'elements' in a total, but when we use any of these words we must remember that we are talking of activities."

~DA195

Leadership as Integrating

"In other words the leader of our neighborhood group must interpret our experience to us, must see all the different points of view which underlie our daily activities and also their connections, must adjust the varying and often conflicting needs, must lead the group to an understanding of its needs and to a unification of its purpose. He must give form to things vague, things latent, to mere tendencies. He must be able to lead us to wise decisions, not to impose his own wise decisions upon us. We need leaders, not masters or drivers."
~NS229

"We see this clearly in international relations. We shall never be able to make an international settlement and erect some power to enforce it; the settlement must be such as to provide its own momentum. A political scientist says in a recent book that authority coordinates the experience of men. It does not. It is just the other way around. Legitimate authority flows from coordination, not co-ordination from authority. This is implied in everything I have said here. Legitimate authority is the interweaving of all the experience concerned."
~DA204

"Legitimate authority is the interweaving of all the experience concerned."
~DA204

4 Following the Invisible Leader

"Yesterday I tried to present to you this conception of leadership. It is a conception very far removed from that of the leader-follower relation. With that conception you had to be either a leader or a leaner. Today our thinking is tending less and less to be confined within the boundaries of those alternatives. There is the idea of a reciprocal leadership. There is also the idea of a partnership in following, of following the invisible leader – the common purpose."
~TS1

"The best executives put this common purpose clearly before their group. While leadership depends on depth of conviction and the power coming there from, there must also be the ability to share that conviction with others, the ability to make purpose articulate. And then that common purpose becomes the leader. And I believe that we are coming more and more to act, whatever our theories, on our faith in the power of this invisible leader. Loyalty to following The Invisible Leader gives us the strongest possible bond of union, establishes a sympathy which is not a sentimental but a dynamic sympathy."
~FC55

"There is also the idea of a partnership in following, of following the invisible leader – the common purpose."
~TS1

"The best executives put this common purpose clearly before their group."
~FC55

"The best leader does not ask people to serve him, but the common end. The best leader has not followers, but men and women working with him. When we find that the leader does less than order and the expert more than advise, subordinates – both executives and workers – will respond differently to leadership. We want to arouse not the attitudes of obedience, but the attitudes of co-operation, and we cannot do that effectively unless we are working for a common purpose understood and defined as such."
~DA262

"But there was another quality which Lincoln possessed, equally necessary for the great leader, one which Woodrow Wilson, for example, did not possess. Woodrow Wilson's ideal of world unity was, I believe, directly in harmony with the spirit of twentieth-century development. Nevertheless, he failed because he could not make America see this. Bismarck could make the German people do what he wanted them to, but his vision was not great enough. Woodrow Wilson, on the other hand, had vision, but could not make enough others see it. Abraham Lincoln is one of the world's greatest leaders because he both had the vision and could share it with others. Therefore what Lincoln accomplished was permanent. It was foundation, other things could be built on it."
~TS139

"The leader releases energy, unites energies, and all with the object not only of carrying out a purpose, but of creating further and larger purposes." ~DA267

4 FINDING THE LAW OF THE SITUATION

Finding the Law of the Situation

"Now what is our problem here? How can we avoid the two extremes: too great bossism in giving orders, and practically no orders given? I am going to ask how you are avoiding these extremes. My solution is to depersonalize the giving of orders, to unite all concerned in a study of the situation, to discover the law of the situation and obey that.

We have here, I think, one of the largest contributions of scientific management: it tends to depersonalize orders. From one point of view, one might call the essence of scientific management the attempt to find the law of the situation.

With scientific management, the managers are as much under orders as the workers, for both obey the law of the situation. Our job is not how to get people to obey orders, but how to devise methods by which we can best *discover* the order integral to a particular situation. When that is found, the employee can issue it to the employer, as well as employer to employee. This often happens easily and naturally. My cook or my stenographer points out the law of the situation, and I, if I recognize it as such, accept it, even although it may reverse some 'order' I have given."

~DA58

Finding the Law of the Situation

"One *person* should not give orders to another *person*, but both should agree to take their orders from the situation."
~DA58

Finding the Law of the Situation

"Integration being the basic law of life, orders should be the composite conclusion of those who give and those who receive them; more than this, that they should be the integration of the people concerned and the situation; more even than this, that they should be the integrations involved in the evolving situation. If you accept my three fundamental statements on this subject: (1) that the order should be the law of the situation; (2) that the situation is always evolving; (3) that orders should involve circular not linear behavior – then we see that our old conception of orders has somewhat changed, and that there should therefore follow definite changes in business practice".
~DA65

"To find the law of the situation rather than to issue arbitrary commands, I have called depersonalising orders. I think it is really a matter of re-personalising. We, persons, have relations with each other, but we should find them in and through the whole situation. We cannot have any sound relations with each other as long as we take them out of the setting which gave them their meaning and value. The divorcing of persons and situation does a great deal of harm. While, therefore, I have said that orders should be depersonalised, a deeper philosophy shows us personal relations within the whole setting of that thing of which they are a part. Within that setting we find the so-called order."

~FC24

4 Leading is Power-With

Leading is Power-With

"Men have long worshipped power; the power of arms, the power of divine right of kings or priests, and then in the nineteenth century the power of majorities. Power is now beginning to be thought of by some as the combined capacities of a group. We get power through effective relations."

~DA248

Leading is Power-With

"So far as my observation has gone, it seems to me that whereas power usually means power-over, the power of some person or group over some other person or group, it is possible to develop the conception of power-with, a jointly developed power, a co-active, not a coercive power. In store or factory I do not think the management should have power *over* the workmen, or the workmen over the management."

~DA101

"I saw recently a statement that when employers admit the right of workers to a share in management, they deliberately give up a part of their freedom. But employers are not 'free' who face strikes, sabotage, dissatisfaction, indifference – all the evils of a condition of struggle between capital and labour. Those employers are the freest who have worked out the means of preventing these evils, and who have found the way of getting from their workers all the possible contributions which they can make to management."
~DA306

Leading is Power-With

"If anyone thinks that the distinction between power-over and power-with is a fanciful or personal distinction, I am pleased to be able to say that these two prepositions are used to mark a distinction in law; you have rights over a slave, you have rights with a servant."
~DA101

"I trust that the difference between this 'equal power', so much talked of, and the power-with we have been considering, is evident. Equal power means the stage set for a fair fight, power-with is a jointly developing power, the aim, a unifying which, while allowing for infinite differing, does away with fighting."
~DA115

Leading is Power-With

"I hope it will be seen that what I have called legitimate power is produced by that circular behavior described in our first talk. Circular behavior is the basis of integration. If your business is so organized that you can influence a co-manager while he is influencing you, so organized that a workman has an opportunity of influencing you as you have of influencing him; if there is an interactive influence going on all the time between you, power-with may be built up. Throughout history we see that control brings disastrous consequences whenever it outruns integration."
~DA104

Leading is Power-With

"For authority, genuine authority, is the outcome of our common life. It does not come from separating people, from dividing them into two classes, those who command and those who obey. It comes from the intermingling of all, of my work fitting into yours and yours into mine, and from that intermingling of forces a power being created which will control those forces. Authority is a self-generating process. To learn more of that process, the process of control, is what we all think the world today most needs."

~FC46

Leading is Power-With

"I do not believe that there will ever come a time when one class has not more power than another, one nation than another, one individual than another. But the more power any one has the better, if we mean by power integrated control. The more the better if it is used to join with the integrated control evolved by other units; we certainly do not want to abolish power, that would be abolishing life itself, but we need a new orientation toward it. The power of the strong is not to be used to conquer the weaker: this means for the conquerors activity which is not legitimately based, which will therefore have disastrous consequences later; and for the conquered, repression."
~CE189

"I have been asked if this is a conservative or a radical point of view. It is both: it is conservative because it is concerned with only actual power, and it takes time and education and training to develop that; it cannot be got by revolution, it involves a process and a slow process; it is concerned with neither granting power nor grabbing power but with evolving power. At the same time it is a radical view because opportunity must be given for this process."
~CE188

Leading is Power-With

"The leader guides the group and is at the same time himself guided by the group, is always a part of the group. No one can truly lead except from within. One danger of conceiving the leader as outside is that then what ought to be group loyalty will become personal loyalty. When we have a leader within the group these two loyalties can merge."

~NS229

"If, then, the essential task of the leader is to free, and since freedom is the result of adjustment, the chief problem of all those who work with human beings is, from one point of view, that of adjustment. It is the problem of the business manager, of the doctor, of the psychiatrist, of the courts, of the legislator and administrator, of the League of Nations. Likewise it is the problem of the teacher. His job is to adjust the individual to life. This is what guides the decisions in regard to the curriculum. The teacher, to be sure, finds the curriculum fixed, but he can at any rate use his judgment to a large extent as to how it should be used. If that is his primary aim – not the giving out of information but the adjustment of the individual to life – he has to know firsthand a good deal about the life to which the individual should be adjusted.

For he may be adjusting the student not to actual conditions, but to imagined conditions, conditions of the past which no longer exist."
~TS2-3

Leading is Power-With

"To sum up our consideration of power-over. Power-over can be reduced: (1) through integration, (2) through recognizing that all should submit to what I have called the law of the situation, and (3) through making our business more and more of a functional unity. In a functional unity each has his function-and that should correspond as exactly as possible with his capacity-and then he should have the authority and the responsibility which go with that function."

~DA106

4 Empowering Functional Leadership

Empowering Functional Leadership

"We have three kinds of leadership: the leadership of position, the leadership of personality and the leadership of function. My claim for modern industry is that in the best managed plants the leadership of function is tending to have more weight and the leadership of mere position or of mere personality less."
~FC58

"There is a growing recognition among business men that there are many different degrees of leadership, that many people have *some* capacity for leadership even although it be of the smallest. And the men who recognize this are trying to work out a form of organization and methods of management which will make the most effective use of such leadership capacity. It is also recognized that there are different types of leadership. I mean not only that there are different leadership qualities possessed by different men, but also that different situations require different kinds of knowledge, and the man possessing the knowledge demanded by a certain situation tends in the best managed businesses, and other things being equal, to become the leader at that moment."
~DA277

"If the best leader takes all the means in his power to develop leadership among his subordinates and gives them opportunity to exercise it, he has then, his supreme task, to unite all the different degrees and different types of leadership that come to the surface in the ramifications of modern business."

~DA282

"We often see individual leadership, that is, leadership irrespective of position, springing up in a committee. There was an instance of this in a sales committee. The chairman of the committee was the sales manager, Smith. Smith was narrow but not obstinate. Not being obstinate, Jones was able to get Smith to soften his opinion on the particular matter in question, and there was then an integration of the opinion of that committee around Jones' leadership."

~FC51

Empowering Functional Leadership

"I think it is of great importance to recognise that leadership is sometimes in one place and sometimes in another. For it tends to prevent apathy among under-executives. It makes them much more alert if they realise that they have many chances of leadership before they are advanced to positions which carry with them definitely, officially, leadership. Moreover, if such occasional leadership is exercised with moderation without claiming too much for oneself, without encroaching on anyone's official position, it may mean that that person will be advanced to an official position of leadership."

~FC51

"The chief thing I have wanted to do in this hour is to explode a long held superstition. We have heard repeated again and again in the past, 'Leaders are born, not made'. I read the other day 'Leadership is a capacity that cannot be acquired'. I believe that leadership can, in part, be learned. I hope you will not let anyone persuade you that it cannot be. The man who thinks leadership cannot be learned will probably remain in a subordinate position. The man who believes he can be, will go to work and learn it. He may not ever be president of the company, but he can rise from where he is.

Moreover, if leadership could not be learned, our large, complex businesses would not have much chance of success, for they require able leadership in many places, not only in the president's chair."

~FC58

4 LEADING BY EXAMPLE

"And do not think that I underestimate the importance of the man at the top. No one could put more importance on top leadership than I do.

I most certainly believe that many personal qualities enter into leadership tenacity, sincerity, fair dealings with all, steadfastness of purpose, depth of conviction, control of temper, tact, steadiness in stormy periods, ability to meet emergencies, power to draw forth and develop the latent possibilities of others, and so on. There are many more. There is, for instance, the force of example on which we cannot lay too great stress. If workers have to work overtime, their head should be willing to do the same. In every way he must show that he is willing to do what he urges on others.

One winter I went yachting with some friends in the inland waterways of the southern part of the United States. On one occasion our pilot led us astray and we found ourselves one night aground in a Carolina swamp. Obviously the only thing to do was to try to push the boat off, but the crew refused, saying that the swamps in that region were infested with rattlesnakes. The owner of the yacht offered not a word of remonstrance, but turned instantly and jumped overboard. Every member of the crew followed."

~FC57

Leading by Example

"The best leaders get their orders obeyed because they too are obeying. Sincerity more than aggressiveness is a quality of leadership."
~FC56

4 LEADERS DEVELOP LEADERS

Leaders Develop Leaders

"Many are coming to think that the job of a man higher up is not to make decisions for his subordinates but to teach them how to handle their problems themselves, teach them how to make their own decisions. The best leader does not persuade men to follow his will. He shows them what it is necessary for them to do in order to meet their responsibility, a responsibility which has been explicitly defined to them. Such a leader is not one who wishes to do people's thinking for them, but one who trains them to think for themselves."
~FC56

"Indeed the best leaders try to train their followers themselves to become leaders. A second-rate executive will often try to suppress leadership because he fears it may rival his own. I have seen several instances of this. But the first-rate executive tries to develop leadership in those under him. He does not want men who are subservient to him, men who render him an unthinking obedience. While therefore there are still men who try to surround themselves with docile servants – you all know that type – the ablest men today have a larger aim, they wish to be leaders of leaders. This does not mean that they abandon one iota of power. But the great leader tries also to develop power wherever he can among those who work with him, and then he gathers all this power and uses it as the energising force of a progressing enterprise."
~FC56

Leaders Develop Leaders

"He is a leader who gives form to the inchoate energy in every man. The person who influences me most is not he who does great deeds but he who makes me feel I can do great deeds. Many people tell me what I ought to do and just how I ought to do it, but few have made me want to do something. Who ever has struck fire out of me, aroused me to action which I should not otherwise have taken, he has been my leader. The community leader is he who can liberate the greatest amount of energy in his community."

~NS230

"The person who influences me most is not he who does great deeds but he who makes me feel I can do great deeds."
~NS230

Leaders Develop Leaders

"I believe that the great leader can show me this correspondence between my capacities and the demands of the universe, can arouse my latent possibilities, can reveal to me new powers in myself, can quicken and give direction to some force within me. There is energy, passion, unawakened life in us – those who call it forth are our leaders."

~DA293

4 LEADERSHIP AND COLLECTIVE CREATIVITY

"In the field of politics we see little to encourage us; but in the League of Nations, in the co-operatives, above all in business administration, we see an appreciation emerging, not in words but in deeds, of what collective creativeness might mean to the world. Much of our theoretical writing accepts without analysis time-honoured phrases and notions, treats as fundamental ideas the crude, primitive attempts to get at democracy by rule of thumb. The world has long been fumbling for democracy, but has not yet grasped its essential and basic idea. Business and industrial organization is, I believe, on the verge of making large contributions to something far more important than democracy, democracy in its more superficial meaning – to the development of integrative unity. Business cannot serve its maximum degree of usefulness to the community, cannot perform the service which it has, tacitly, *bound* itself to perform, unless it seeks an enlarged understanding of the practical methods of unifying business organization."
~DA94

"The period of *laissez-faire* is indeed over, but I do not think we want to put in its place a forcibly controlled society, whether it be controlled by the state of the socialists or the experts of a planning board. The aim and the process of the organisation of government, of industry, of international relations, should be, I think, a control not imposed from without the regular functioning of society, but one which is a co-ordinating of all those functions, that is, a collective self-control."

~FC88

"If then you accept my definition of control as a self-generating process, as the interweaving experience of all those who are performing a functional part of the activity under consideration, does not that constitute an imperative? Are we not every one of us bound to take some part consciously in this process? Today we are slaves to the chaos in which we are living. To get our affairs in hand, to feel a grip on them, to become free, we must learn, and practice, I am sure, the methods of collective control. To this task we can all devote ourselves. At the same time that we are selling goods or making goods, or whatever we are doing, we can be working in harmony with this fundamental law of life. We can be aware that by this method control is in our power."
~FC89

"Through neighborhood organization we hope that real leaders instead of bosses will be evolved. Democracy does not tend to suppress leadership as is often stated; it is the only organization of society which will bring out leadership. As soon as we are given opportunities for the release of the energy there is in us, heroes and leaders will arise among us. These will draw their stimulus, their passion, their life from all, and then in their turn increase in all passion and power and creating force."
~NS231

"Our officials in their campaign speeches say that they are the 'servants of the people.' But we do not want 'servants' any more than we want bosses; we want genuine leaders. Now that more and more direct power is being given to the people it is especially necessary that we should not be led by machine bosses, but that we should evolve the kind of leadership which will serve a true democracy, which will be the expression of a true democracy, and will guide it to democratic ends by democratic methods."
~NS227

5

Mary Parker Follett on Democracy

> *"Indeed, it has been said that democracy is the worst form of Government except all those other forms that have been tried from time to time."*
> ~ Winston Churchill, said in House of Commons, November 11, 1947.

The failure of some of today's democracies is striking. In many countries, representative democracy has shown its limits. Government projects are blocked while their design and validation have strictly followed the rules of so-called "democratic process". Many crises today reveal the loss of faith in our present attempts at democracy: the Occupy movement, the rise of extremist parties, etc.

Beyond ballot boxes, voting, and the majority rule as guiding principles of our democracy in action, Follett suggests a breakthrough method. The democratic solution is not what the crowd or what the majority agrees on, it is the behavioral capacity to co-create an authentic collective will. Not a collective will that is a mere compromise, but rather a completely new will. An integration of individual wills into something greater.

Contrary to the strictly institutional understanding of democracy, the idea of democracy proposed by Follett leads to the emergence of a social conscience. An awareness of living in interdependence and a belief that to become fully human means participating and contributing one's full self to the co-creation of one's common life.

The idea of democracy is more than just a new form of political institution. It is a plea for a new method of living together.

Follett's perspective on the notion of democracy is presented here through these five sub-categories of quotes.

1. New method, new democracy

This first section deals with the breakthrough that Mary Parker Follett introduced: a system that produces the social will, more than simply a system based on individual expression.

2. Learning democracy

There is no natural sense of democracy. It must be learned.

3. Creating rather than following

Rights are not given. Ideals are not just sealed-up into safety boxes. Rights and ideals are co-created and by this process give birth to social consciousness.

4. Democracy, patriotism and loyalty

Patriotism according to Follett means you belong to a nation because you participate in making that nation. You belong to a group because you participate in creating that group.

5. Living democracy

Follett defends a certain conception of democracy: not just a plea for a new political system, but a plea for a new consciousness for wholeness.

5 New Method, New Democracy

New Method, New Democracy

"All our ideas of conscious self-determination lead us to a new method: it is not merely that we must be allowed to govern ourselves, we must learn how to govern ourselves; it is not only that we must be given 'free speech', we must learn a speech that is free; we are not given rights, we create rights; it is not only that we must invent machinery to get a social will expressed, we must invent machinery that will get a social will created."

~NS8-9

New Method, New Democracy

"But method must not connote mechanics to any mind. Many of us are more interested in the mechanisms of life than in anything else. We keep on putting pennies in the slot from sheer delight in seeing something come out at the other end. All this must change. Machines, forms, images, moulds – all must be broken up and the way prepared for our plastic life to find plastic expression. The principle of democracy may be the underlying unity of men, the method of democracy must be that which allows the quickest response of our daily life to the common faith of men."

~NS4

New Method, New Democracy

"Politics do not need to be 'purified'. This thought is leading us astray. Politics must be vitalized by new method. 'Representative government', party organization, majority rule, with all their excrescences, are deadwood. In their stead must appear the organization of non-partisan groups for the begetting, the bringing into being, of common ideas, a common purpose and a collective will."
~NS4

"The world has long been fumbling for democracy, but has not yet grasped its essential and basic idea."

~DA94

New Method, New Democracy

"The study of democracy has been based largely on the study of institutions; it should be based on the study of how men behave together. We have to deal, not with institutions, or any mechanical thing, or with abstract ideas, or 'man,' or anything but just men, ordinary men. The importance of the new psychology is that it acknowledges man as the center and shaper of his universe. In his nature all institutions are latent and perforce must be adapted to this nature. Man not things must be the starting point of the future."
~NS19

"We talk about the tragedy of individualism. The individual we do not yet know, for we have no methods to release the powers of the individual. Our particularism – our *laissez-faire*, our every-man-for-his-own-interests – has little to do with true individualism, that is, with the individual as consciously responsible for the life from which he draws his breath and to which he contributes his all."
~NS3

"Democracy does not mean being lost in the mass, it means the contribution of every power I possess to social uses. The individual is not lost in the whole, he makes the whole."
~NS337

"The expert must find his place within the social process; he can never be made a substitute for it. Technical experience must be made a part of all the available experience. When we see expert and administrative official, legislator and judge, *and* the people, all integral parts of the social process, all learning how to make facts, how to view facts, how to develop criteria by which to judge facts, then only have we have a vision of a genuine democracy. We have not to choose between becoming an expert on every subject ourselves and swallowing whole the reports of experts. The training of the citizen must include both how to form opinion on expert testimony and how to watch one's own experience and draw conclusions from it."
~CE29

New Method, New Democracy

"The problem of democracy is how to develop power from experience, from the interplay of our daily concrete activities. The expert cannot dictate and the people consent. We might be told here that we need from the expert the facts by which to understand the tariff. Certainly, but we need just as much a method for connecting those facts with our own lives."

~CE197

"There is no above and below. We cannot schematize men as space objects. The study of community as process will bring us, I believe, not to the over-individual mind, but to the inter-individual mind, an entirely different conception."
~CP5836

5 Learning Democracy

"The training for the new democracy must be from the cradle – through nursery, school and play, and on and on through every activity of our life. Citizenship is not to be learned in good government classes or current events courses or lessons in civics. It is to be acquired only through those modes of living and acting which shall teach us how to grow the social consciousness. This should be the object of all day school education, of all night school education, of all our supervised recreation, of all our family life, of our club life, of our civic life."
~NS363

5 Creating Rather than Following

Creating Rather than Following

"We do not follow right merely, we create right. It is often thought vaguely that our ideals are all there, shining and splendid, and we have only to apply them. But the truth is that we have to create our ideals. No ideal is worthwhile which does not grow from our actual life. Some people seem to keep their ideals all carefully packed away from dust and air, but arranged alphabetically so that they can get at them quickly in need. But we can never take out a past ideal for a present need. The ideal which is to be used for our life must come out from that very life itself. The only way our past ideals can help us is in molding the life which produces the present ideal; we have no further use of them. But we do not discard them: we have built them into the present, we have used them up as the cocoon is used up in making the silk. It has been sometimes taught that given the same situation, the individual must repeat the same behavior. But the situation is never the same, the individual is never the same; such a conception has nothing to do with life. We cannot do our duty in the old sense, that is following a crystallized ideal, because our duty is new at every moment."
~NS52

Creating Rather than Following

"When the ought is not a mandate from without, it is no longer a prohibition but a self-expression. As the social consciousness develops, ought will be swallowed up in will. We are some time truly to see our life as positive, not negative, as made up of continuous willing, not of restraints and prohibition. Morality is not the refraining from doing certain things, it is a constructive force."
~NS53

"As the social consciousness develops, ought will be swallowed up in will."
~NS53

"The source of the binding power of law is not in the consent of the community, but in the fact that it has been produced by the community."
~NS130

"The state accumulates moral power only through the spiritual activity of its citizens. There is no state except through me. James' deep-seated antagonism to the idealists is because of their assertion that the absolute is, always has been and always will be. The contribution of pragmatism is that we must work out the absolute. You are drugging yourselves, cries James, the absolute is real as far as you make it real, as far as you bring forth in tangible, concrete form all its potentialities.

In the same way we have no state until we make one. This is the teaching of the new psychology. We have not to 'postulate' all sorts of things as the philosophers do ('organic actuality of the moral order' etc.), we have to *live* it; if we can make a moral whole then we shall know whether or not there is one. We cannot become the state imaginatively, but only actually through our group relations. Stamped with the image of All-State-potentiality we must be forever making the state. We are pragmatists in politics as the new school of philosophy is in religion: just as they say that we are one with God not by prayer and communion alone, but by doing the God-deed every moment, so we are one with the state by actualizing the latent state at every instant of our lives. As God appears only through us, so is the state made visible through the political man. We must gird up our loins, we must light our lamp and set forth, we must *do* it."

~NS334-335

"The only unity or community is one we have made of ourselves, by ourselves, for ourselves."
~NS59

"A democratic community is one in which the common will is being gradually created by the civic activity of its citizens."
~NS51

Creating Rather than Following

"It is often thought that when some restraint is taken away from us we are freer than before, but this is childish. Some women-suffragists talk of women as 'enslaved' and advocate their emancipation by the method of giving them the vote. But the vote will not make women free. Freedom is always a thing to be attained. And we must remember too that freedom is not a static condition. As it is not something possessed 'originally', and as it is not something which can be given to us, so also it is not something won once for all. It is in our power to win our freedom, but it must be won anew at every moment, literally every moment. People think of themselves as not free because they think of themselves as obeying some external law, but the truth is we are the lawmakers. My freedom is my share in creating, my part in the creative responsibility. The heart of our freedom is the impelling power of the will of the whole. Who then are free? Those who win their freedom through fellowship."
~NS71-72

"Some writers talk of social justice as if a definite idea of it existed, and that all we have to do to regenerate society is to direct our efforts towards the realization of this ideal. But the ideal of social justice is itself a collective and a progressive development, that is, it is produced through our associated life and it is produced anew from day to day. We do not want a 'perfect' law to regulate the hours of women in industry; we want that kind of life which will make us, all of us, grow the best ideas about the hours of women in industry, about women in industry, about women, about industry."
~NS130

Creating Rather than Following

"We cannot assume that we possess a body of achieved ideas stamped in some mysterious way with the authority of reason and justice, but even were it true, the reason and justice of the past must give way to the reason and justice of the present. You cannot bottle up wisdom – it won't keep – but through our associated life it may be distilled afresh at every instant. We are coming now to see indeed that law is a social imperative in the strict psychological sense, that is, that it gets its authority through the power of group life."

~NS130-131

Creating Rather than Following

"To sum up this point: morality is never static; it advances as life advances. You cannot hang your ideals up on pegs and take down no. 2 for certain emergencies and no. 4 for others. *The true test of our morality is not the rigidity with which we adhere to standard, but the loyalty we show to the life which constructs standards.* The test of our morality is whether we are living not to follow but to create ideals, whether we are pouring our life into our visions only to receive it back with its miraculous enhancement for new uses."

~NS54-55

5 Democracy, Patriotism and Loyalty

"Perhaps one of the most useful lessons to be learned from the group process is a new definition of patriotism. Patriotism must not be herd-instinct. Patriotism must be the individual's rational, self-conscious building of his country every moment. Loyalty means always to create your group, not to wave a flag over it. We need a patriotism which is not 'following the lead' but involved in a process in which all take part. In the place of sentimental patriotism we want a common purpose, a purpose evolved by the common life, to be used for the common life.

~NS346

"Some of our biologists mislead us when they talk of the homogeneity of the herd as the aim of nations. The nation may be a herd at present. What we have to do is to make it a true group. Internationalism must be based upon group units, not upon herd or crowd units, that is, upon people united not by herd instinct but by group conviction. If a nation is a crowd, patriotism is mere hypnotism; if a nation is a true federal state built up of interlocking and ascending groups, then patriotism is self-evolved. When you are building up an association or a nation you have to preach loyalty; later it is part of the very substance which has been built. Then genuine loyalty, a self-evolved loyalty, will always lead the way to higher units."

~NS346-347

"If a nation is a crowd,
patriotism is mere hypnotism."
~NS346

"When we understand the principle of unifying taught by the latest psychology and the oldest philosophy, we shall no longer fear the state or deify the state. The state, as state, is not the supreme object of my allegiance. The supreme object of my allegiance is never a thing, a made. It is the very Process itself to which I give my loyalty and every activity of my life."
~CP6

"The 'good citizen' is not he who obeys the laws, but he who has an active sense of being an integral part of the state. This is the essence and the basis of effective good citizenship. We are not part of a nation because we are living within its boundaries, because we feel in sympathy with it and have accepted its ideas, because we have become naturalized. We are part of a nation only in so far as we are helping to make that nation."

~NS339

5 Living Democracy

"There has gradually come into the world a new idea of democracy... if we here tonight pledge ourselves to the new democracy, a new force will be created in the world. For we no longer think of democracy as a form of government. We know now that it is far more than that. It is the substance of life. It is the flame at the heart of man, the flame which binds us together, makes us one, not many. Democracy is not a goal, it is the path; it is not attainment, but a process. It is the 'more abundant life'. It is the attitude of man towards his fellow-man. It is the only true method of living. When we once grasp this and begin to live democracy, then only shall we have democracy."
~SC14-15

"Democracy is an infinitely including spirit. We have an instinct for democracy because we have an instinct for wholeness; we get wholeness only through reciprocal relations, through infinitely expanding reciprocal relations"
~NS157

Living Democracy

"Let us joyously do the work of the world because we are the world. Such is the *élan de vie*, the joy of high activity, which leaps forward with force, in freedom."
~NS71

Mary Parker Follett (1868-1933)

Image from Lyndall Urwick's *The Golden Book of Management: A Historical Record of the Life and Work of Seventy Pioneers.* 1956. London: N. Neame.

Bibliography

~CE *Creative Experience*. 1924. New York: Longmans, Green and Co.

~CP *Community is a Process*. Article published in *Philosophical Review*, Vol. XXVIII, 1919, pp. 576-88.

~DA *Dynamic Administration: The Collected Papers of Mary Parker Follett*. 1941. London: Pitman and Sons Ltd. Edited by Henry Metcalf and Lyndall Urwick.

~FC *Freedom & Co-ordination: Lectures in Business Organization*. 1949. London: Management Publications Trust Ltd. Edited by Lyndall Urwick.

~NS *The New State – Group Organization, The Solution of Popular Government*. 1918. New York: Longmans, Green and Co.

~SC *The Social Centre and the Democratic Ideal*. Paper presented on December 14, 1913 at Ford Hall Forum, Boston.

~TS *The Teacher-Student Relation*. Salvaged Address given by Follett at Boston University in 1928 and first published in *Administrative Science Quarterly* in 1970.

Acknowledgments

The first person our group wishes to acknowledge is recently deceased Professor John Hoang Sarvey, former executive director of Northeastern University's School of Public Policy and Urban Affairs in Boston. A passionate student of Mary Parker Follett, John hosted our first Follett Conversations at Northeastern in the fall of 2011. This allowed our group to meet in person for the first time. Thanks, John, for being part of this *élan de vie*, we miss you.

Our thanks also go to Pauline Graham and Joan Tonn who have paved the way for contemporary explorers of Mary Parker Follett. We continue in their footsteps.

Anne Coyle participated in our group and generously contributed her time and shared her thoughts, knowledge and passion for Mary Parker Follett.

While our group worked regularly through our Sunday internet conference calls, we also needed to meet physically and spend time co-creating this work together. Our thanks to the Université de Rouen and Sébastien Damart for hosting our first working session in the fall of 2012 and for supporting our project along the way.

The following summer we had the privilege of renting Rudyard Kipling's former home, Naulakha, near Mary Parker Follett's former country home in Putney, Vermont, thanks to Landmark Trust USA. Naulakha was a magical space to meet, work and dream this intellectual project together.

In the fall of 2013, Belgian professor and practitioner in organizational change and leadership Herman Wittockx generously offered us the use of Hubermont, "Space for Development", in the beautiful region of the Ardennes. Hubermont's spacious setting was also conducive to our collaborative efforts. It was Herman who made us appreciate the poetic quality of some of Follett's words. Danku Herman!

Spring of 2014, Albie's daughter Michelle Davis, while on a family trip, offered us their beautiful Boston home for our third face-to-face work session. The walls filled with books were an inspiring environment to work in. Thanks so much Michelle!

And we thank Ben Davis, Albie Davis' son, for being our first official supporter. Thanks, Ben, for being there from the beginning. It made a difference!

The aesthetic quality of this book has been of great importance to us and we have been blessed to have Carole Zabbal-Wynne generously add her magic touch on your reading experience of this book.

A special thank you

This book has been the fruit of so many genuine efforts to make Mary Parker Follett's voice better appreciated and applied.

Several readers from a variety of backgrounds, countries, and points of view have enriched our work with their advice.

We thank them for their generosity.

Sonia Adam-Ledunois (France)

Lucile Beaubien (Canada)

Josefine Biedermann (Germany)

Laurent Chartier (Canada)

Laïla Chraïbi (Canada)

Colette Damart (France)

Benjamin Davis (USA)

Ronald Fry (USA)

Véronique Gingras (Canada)

Pauline Graham (UK)

Franke Jongsma (The Netherlands)

Gurudev Khalsa (USA)

David Kolb (USA)

Fatima Zohra Makhtoum (Canada)

Susan Mawer (UK)

Manulani Aluli Meyer (Aotearoa/New Zealand)

Lisa Nelson (USA)

Prabha Packiam (Canada)

Ana Schofield (USA)

Peter Spence (Australia)

David Steingard (USA)

Tojo Thatchenkery (USA)

Judy Watkins (USA)

Herman Wittockx (Belgium)

About the Editors

*Under the Kipling spell in Naulakha (L-R):
Jennifer Jones-Patulli, François Héon,
Albie Davis, Anne Coyle, and Sébastien Damart.
Photo © Sébastien Damart*

Jennifer Jones-Patulli

Professional mediator, conflict coach and organizational consultant, Jennifer Jones-Patulli is inspired by the creative potential in conflict. Finding Follett while completing a Master's degree in Conflict Studies, she continues to apply the concept of integrative behavior to resolving interpersonal and group conflict in the workplace.

jennifer.jones.patulli@gmail.com

François Héon

Organizational psychologist and leadership consultant François was first introduced to Mary Parker Follett by late Suresh Srivastva, professor of organizational behavior. Follett's ideas have since become a beacon of wisdom in his international practice and personal life.

✉ *fheon@francoisheon.com*

Albie Davis

"Follett never ceases to amaze me," says Albie Davis, former Director of Mediation for the District Courts of Massachusetts. Davis has offered mediation "training for trainers" in the U.S., Canada, Australia, South Africa and Hungary, where a four-country team worked with teachers from 20 countries, including Russia, Kazakhstan, Bosnia, and the Czech Republic. Davis delights in how quickly people the world over grasp Follett's ideas on making democracy work – then together create their own innovations -- soaring to new heights.

✉ *albiedavis@aol.com*

Sébastien Damart

Professor at Paris-Dauphine University, PSL Research University and organization consultant, Sébastien Damart brought a wealth of knowledge and consulting experience in applying Mary Parker Follett principles to management. His recent applications of "Integrative Management" à la Follett to healthcare organizations has been an inspiring source of managerial innovations.

sebastien.damart@gmail.com

The editors would like to acknowledge the invaluable assistance and contributions of Anne Coyle to this project. Thank you, Anne. This book would not have been the same without your involvement.